"Jennie could not ... smothered in God': ... I am her mother! I ... her pilgrimage from ... God's sufficiency over and over again. A perusal through her book is equivalent to reliving some of the lowest points and the deepest pains of the past few years of my daughter's existence, with the most exhilarating realization that her faith in God filled in every gap and every shortage with incredible provision and sustenance.

If you are facing the worst season of your life, or you just want to rejoice in the faithfulness of your heavenly Father, then arm yourself with a box of tissues, find a cozy place with a lamp to light your way through the next few hours, and crack open *Just Enough* for an adventurous ride towards accelerated faith, fueled by hope, and guided by grace. It is a journey you will long remember and want to share with others who may need a boost along the way."

Ruth Puleo, director of PennDel Women of Purpose, minister, former associate pastor, missionary evangelist, writer, speaker, and proud mother of Jennie Puleo

"In her new book, *Just Enough,* Jennie Puleo is transparent and truthful about the difficult pathway she was forced to walk after enduring a life-altering betrayal. Her book is a joyful and hope-drenched reminder that even if others are unfaithful, God is always faithful; if others abandon us, God never does. Her life is living proof that God will supply whatever we need at the very moment we need it".

Marie Armenia, conference speaker, songwriter and author of *The Audacious Molly Bruno*

"In her new book, *Just Enough,* Jennie expresses raw emotions with authentic grace and profound truths evidenced through the darkest moments; truly inspiring! Her touching stories are demonstrated by God's hand in the most unexpected places. Definitely a must read, and seriously, make sure to have tissues close by!"

Cristin Germaine, speaker & co-author of *The Beauty In MY Mess*

"When life is messy, confusing, and riddled with pain, it's difficult to hear God's voice. With refreshing honesty, Jennie shares her story of overcoming heart-wrenching adversity and discovering true healing. Through her deeply impacting message, we, too, find the strength we need to choose faith and experience freedom."

Angela Donadio, author of *Finding Joy When Life is Out of Focus: Philippians - A Study for Joy-Thirsty Women,* Ordained Assemblies of God minister

"Tears have found a way to escape the depths of my soul and seep through my heart while reading this real-life story of faith, courage, healing and letting go. *Just Enough* is practically truth-piercing with a saving grace that reality cannot shake. In the midst of trauma and the everyday battles that we face, it is a pleasant reminder of God's pursuit to show Himself faithful in our times of pain and brokenness. Jennie Puleo's gift to communicate the unthinkable is both courageous and inspiring. I applaud her strength and transparency as she seeks to offer hope to all those who read it."

Shonda White, volunteer staff coordinator for The Refuge Church, former educator & freelance writer

"Jennie Puleo has shown us through *Just Enough* the resilience of the human spirit when completely reliant upon a sovereign God. Reading her story will not only build your faith in The Great Provider but will also remind you of the importance of a Jesus-community to surround you.

As we see the story unfold, she paints a picture of complete hopelessness after betrayal and the rebuilding of a beautiful life. Jesus met her exactly where she needed Him and held her family in his victorious right hand.

Jennie's life stands as a testimony to all of us that when adversity hits our lives, we can make it! I cried, I laughed, I got angry, and I closed the book with a greater respect for Jennie and a higher resolve to live my life connected to Jesus!"

Sheila L. Harper, founder and president of SaveOne

"It's not every day you watch someone walk through the mountains and the valleys of life with such grace and poise. It is inspiring to journey with someone as they feel the sting of loss, rejection, and grief, and yet, they continue to trust and lean on Jesus—their true source of life, strength, and joy for all they need! I have had the privilege of being Jen's friend for many years, and I've seen her live out the contents of this Holy Spirit-inspired book. Reading Jen's heart will encourage you as you reflect on your own journey, and I'm confident you too will see that God has and will always provide *"Just Enough"* of all you need."

Jessica Davis, speaker

Just Enough

Grace. Provision. Hope.

JENNIE PULEO

May you always have Just Enough!

♡, Jen Puleo

UNITED ➤ HOUSE

ISBN 978-1-7327194-0-8

UNITED HOUSE Publishing
Clarkston, Michigan
info@unitedhousepublishing.com
www.unitedhousepublishing.com

Cover design: Cara Lawson, caralawsondesign@gmail.com
Cover photography: Talia Puleo
Interior design: Shawna Johnson

Printed in the United States of America
2018—First Edition

SPECIAL SALES
Most UNITED HOUSE books are available at special quantity discounts when purchased in bulk by corporations, organizations, and special-interest groups. For information, please e-mail orders@unitedhousepublishing.com

I would not be where I am or who I am without the steady and persistent presence of Jesus Christ in my life. I am daily grateful for how He has carried me, guided me, and sustained me through the most difficult and heart-breaking circumstances I've ever known. Without Him, I would have nothing of value to write, and I credit Him for the words penned on each page of this book.

Contents.

Prologue.

Those big brown eyes; ever-watching, seeking truth, looking for hope and security. They were a reflection of my own desire for understanding and encouragement. What Natalia was searching for in me, I was looking to God for the same thing. We both needed to hear, "It's gonna be ok," "This will all work out," "You're gonna make it," "This isn't the end of your story."

Shortly after Natalia and I moved in with my parents, I opened my Bible in desperation for truth and hope. I needed to know God was with me; that He was going to provide for me and my daughter despite our limited resources. I didn't know where to even begin reading, so I randomly picked a page and landed in 1 Kings 17.

> Then the LORD said to Elijah, "Go and live in the village of Zarephath, near the city of Sidon. I have instructed a widow there to feed you."
> So he went to Zarephath. As he arrived at the gates of the village, he saw a widow gathering sticks, and he asked her, "Would you please bring me a little water in a

cup?" As she was going to get it, he called to her, "Bring
me a bite of bread, too."
But she said, "I swear by the LORD your God that I don't
have a single piece of bread in the house. And I have
only a handful of flour left in the jar and a little cooking oil
in the bottom of the jug. I was just gathering a few sticks
to cook this last meal, and then my son and I will die."
But Elijah said to her, "Don't be afraid! Go ahead and do
just what you've said, but make a little bread for me first.
Then use what's left to prepare a meal for yourself and
your son. For this is what the LORD, the God of Israel,
says: There will always be flour and olive oil left in your
containers until the time when the LORD sends rain and
the crops grow again!"
So she did as Elijah said, and she and Elijah and her
family continued to eat for many days. There was always
ENOUGH flour and olive oil left in the containers, just as
the LORD had promised through Elijah.
(1 Kings 17:8, emphasis added)

As I read, it was as though this story leapt off the page and hit me between the eyes. The same promise spoken to the widow—that she would always have enough—was the same promise I believed God was speaking to me.

A few days later, as I tucked my daughter into bed, she asked a string of questions that revealed her fear for our future and need for peace. "How are we going to afford to live on our own without Daddy's money?" "How will we be able to buy food or live in our own house?" "What will we do if you can't work?" These were all the same questions I had been asking of God when He led me to the story of the widow. So I took that moment to read the same story to Natalia.

With great conviction and peace, I was able to assure her that I believed God was telling me that we would always have what we needed when we needed it. That we did not need to fear because God was our provider and He was going to take care of us. I didn't know "how," but I knew "Who."

Trust had been broken. And trust needed to be rebuilt. Everything we thought we could trust, we couldn't. Everything we thought was, wasn't. We were starting over. Though God hadn't been the one to break my trust, He understood that my ability to trust was shaky, and He was willing to do the work to build my capacity to trust Him—in everything.

This process wasn't easy. Honestly, learning total dependence on God has been the hardest journey of my life. Letting go of control, for a control-freak, is a painful process. But putting my trust in Him completely has been the most freeing experience, and I live with more peace now than ever before.

I faced many uncertainties, unknowns, and challenges; times when I literally didn't know how we would survive. Through it all, every step of the way, God proved that we would always have JUST ENOUGH.

1

Unfolding Grace.

I stood in the center of the living room in my beautiful, circa 1925 craftsman-style home and began to survey the losses. Within three days, I managed to sell most of the furniture in my home and chose to keep only the pieces that were family heirlooms. My mind transported me to another time as I stared at the handcrafted wood mantel and brick fireplace with built-in wooden storage benches on either side. I thought of the toys and board games that used to be stored in those benches; games that our little family of three played in that living room, sharing snacks and plenty of laughs. Movie nights snuggled on the couch, grabbing handfuls of my "Special Popcorn," made with my own recipe of sweet and salty goodness, from a giant bowl. For a moment, it was like we were together, sitting in front of the tree on Christmas morning, donned in our brand new jammies we had opened Christmas Eve, sipping our cups of hot cocoa and opening presents with a fire burning.

Broken memories.

Memories that once brought joy and comfort were suddenly laced with grief and a poignantly sharp pain to my chest. My head spun at how sweet memories instantly became so bitter.

Suddenly, I was jerked back into reality as a friend asked me if the contents of the box she was holding were being packed in the trailer or going to storage. Another friend from church crossed my line of view to the fireplace with boxes in hand. Movement was all around me; women from our local church, who were dear friends, packed boxes and moved my belongings from one room to another. They sought my direction, and I responded almost on autopilot. Somehow, I was able to make clear decisions with little thought at all.

GRACE.

It was there, even in the pain.

My energy had drained. I ate only because I knew I had to in order to maintain life. Bless the women who tried to help me remember this as they worked tirelessly to pack each item with care and encouraged me to sit, direct, and try to eat something.

I tried to stay focused, give orders, and remain on task, but each item they held up contained memories, all good ones now tainted with bitterness. The pain was building up within me. I could see similar pain and sympathy reflected in each of my precious friends' eyes. It eventually became too overwhelming to look at them, so my eyes were now fixed on the bowl of soup that was handed to me.

Eat. You need to eat.

I stared at the little, white, Styrofoam bowl as though it was all that existed. I thought the world would fade away around me if I just stared deep enough into the bowl or looked long enough at the contents of soup. The more I stared, however, the higher the pain rose in my chest, then tightened in my throat and poured out of my eyes. The dam holding back the emotion had suddenly burst. I couldn't hold it back any longer. It was impossible to stay on task as this wave of grief crashed down on me. Apparently, this was also true for the eight or so other ladies working in the kitchen and dining room. As I lowered my emotional guard and let sobs break through, these women surrounded me and joined me in the release of tears. My friend, Melissa, even said through sobs, "I was wondering how long I was going to have to hold this in while you kept it together."

There is something sacred about letting tears flow in the presence of those who are genuinely grieving with you, another wave of grace covering me in the middle of the mess.

A month earlier, before I knew of any lies, betrayal, and brokenness in my marriage, I had a conversation with my husband (and only my husband) about what to get our daughter for Christmas. Our (then) seven-year-old daughter was getting more and more into the 18-inch doll craze and was beginning to collect more items for her precious Josephina. (Who looks EXACTLY like her, by the way.)

In our discussion, I asked him if he would be willing to make her a cabinet to store her doll items. He had some woodworking skills, and we tossed around some design ideas that would make the cabinet a furniture piece in her room and have space to hang the doll clothes.

The weeks following that day of tears, friendship, and grace in my kitchen became extremely blurry as my world began to fall apart. I don't remember exactly which day of packing it was or when in the day it occurred, but I do hold the memory of my sweet friend, Abby, stepping into the chaotic living room of boxes, friends, movement, and grief. She was holding a large black garbage bag full of beautiful clothes for my Natalia that would fit her as she grew into the next size and would be perfect for the approaching winter. The provision for an anticipated need was so apparent that it caused my breath to catch in my chest for a moment.

After her brief description of the bagged contents and where they came from, she asked another friend to help her grab something else from the car. I thought nothing of it as people were moving things from here to there and there to here; I had zero sense of where any of my belongings were or where I even was in the middle of it all. Complete chaos. Blurred. Fuzzy.

Just then, the ladies approached the front entryway of the house, and others rushed to assist with the door as I stood there, my movements and reactions set to slow motion. They finagled what they were carrying through the door, and I struggled to be present, to focus. I was trying desperately to grasp why large items were being moved *into* the house while everyone was working to move them *out.* Then, I saw the back of a white cabinet coming toward me, and the girls spun it around for me to see: a beautiful, hand-crafted, white cabinet with two little doors in the center and a drawer below. It was fitted with four pale pink flower knobs and stood about two and a half feet tall.

I'm positive I had an extremely confused look on my face as Abby quickly began to explain what I was seeing. "My grandfather," she said, "had it on his heart to make this for Natalia." A grandfather, mind you, neither my daughter nor I had ever met. She proceeded to pull on the adorable, girly knobs and open the cabinet doors to show me the dowel rod placed inside to hang the 18-inch doll clothes. On it hung an outfit she had sweetly picked out to give Natalia. The drawer also contained items she had gotten for me to be able to give Tali for Christmas!

Right then, in the middle of my vacant living room, fuzzy mind and broken heart, God was silently yelling, "I'm RIGHT here! I'm here in the mess. I'm here in the chaos. I know what's on your heart."

Too emotionally drained to fully react with gratitude or even explain the deep rooted meaning this had for me at that moment,

I'm pretty sure I just stood there, staring: down at the miracle; up at my friend; back down at the miracle. *How could there possibly be a blessing now, when all my heart knew to feel was pain? How is light present in such darkness?* So difficult to understand, and yet it was tangible and I was looking at it.

No matter how difficult the circumstance or how painful the loss, God has been so faithful to remind me of His presence. He doesn't leave us when life gets rough, but sometimes our view of Him is easily clouded by all the emotion and chaos swirling around us. So many lessons were learned, blessings received, and the true nature of God revealed, simply because I was willing to look to Him for help.

2

A Box of Faith.

The week of packing and moving was, and still is, an absolute blur as I struggled to identify and collect enough broken pieces of one life in hopes of rebuilding another... some day. I'm grateful for the grace and wisdom that God kept feeding me in daily doses. I continued looking to Him for answers because I couldn't make any sense of what was happening. Even though I didn't know what I would face next, He was so faithful to give me the wisdom I needed at the right moment. There were times, I admit, where my trust in Him wavered, and I wasn't really sure if, or how, He'd help me through. But by seeing His hand working in my life, He knew I would experience the peace I needed. In so many times and so many ways, He was there.

I knew my daughter and I needed a haven—a place to heal and regroup and have support—but what I really craved was a hole to bury the broken pieces of my heart in or a rock to lie behind and waste away. I was devastated in the truest definition of the word. I couldn't look ahead or envision anything beyond the minute I was desperately trying to live through. The pain was searing and numbing at the same time, and every move I made felt heavy and clunky; it was as though I was feeling my way through the darkness of a cave. It was exhausting. I just wanted to lie down and close my eyes. I wanted to hide. I wanted it all to go away. I yearned to wake up and find out it was all just a terrible nightmare; it wasn't real and I was mistaken. I longed to go back to the security and joy of my little family. Back to laughter and happy memories. Back to things I now realize weren't reality. Everything I believed about my life and my marriage really wasn't truth, but so many lies. So much betrayal. In wishing I could go back, I was reminded of all the reasons I was experiencing my current pain and confusion. I couldn't go back. There was nothing to go back to. Even if my marriage had a miraculous turnaround, we would still have to address what was broken and work to heal what was damaged. My heart hurt and I had so many questions.

For the first time in my life, I was stuck in my present circumstances without the ability to formulate a plan, tidy the mess up, and march on toward the future. I prided myself on my ability to assess a situation, recognize and mend what was damaged, and make a plan to move forward. It's also made me a great nurse. I was capable of not only doing this in my own life, but for others as well. For years, growing up in a pastor's home and then serving as a pastor's wife, I would receive people in their broken places, listen to their stories, and help them determine what they *did* have control over and what they could do next to move beyond their present mess.

My parents recall me answering our parsonage telephone at age nine in a surprisingly professional manner. I would listen to the problem shared by the caller (usually a church member) and often give great advice and encouragement. If it was something that was beyond my knowledge, I would pass on the call to my parents. I was NINE! Triage, damage control, and formulating a plan was my specialty. I had years of experience and practice at it. Now *I* was the one desperately needing someone to come in and just tell me what to do next. I wanted to hear it was all going to be okay, and I was going to make it. I was looking for someone to pick me up, dust me off, mend my heart, and carry me out of the pile of rubble.

There was no HAZMAT team or damage control squad to step in and take over. I was left to navigate life for my daughter and myself on my own. Everything felt so out of control, undone, and uncertain. How easily fear could have taken over; I didn't want to make a wrong move. I wasn't sure what to plan for. I was lacking hope for the future and had no idea what it would look like. I didn't have a job. I was a homeschooling, stay-at-home mom with many physical limitations. I had no source of income or way of supporting my daughter on my own. So many questions. So much unknown. Too much to process while my heart was bleeding out.

In realizing I couldn't go back and had nothing to look forward to, I stood still and looked up. In my thirty years of life, there were so many moments and places God had met me in the past, and I knew He was truly all I had left in this mess. It seemed like I was out of options. I wasn't able to figure this one out. I couldn't clean this up on my own. This situation was beyond my capabilities to manage or redeem. I needed a savior. I was desperate for His help, His strength, His provision. I needed to know He was with me in this and would pull me through.

All I thought I knew meant nothing at this point. I resolved, rather quickly, to let go of my own way of thinking and surrender to simply taking steps as He directed. I was suddenly reminded that although I didn't have control of the people or things around me, I *did* have control of myself and *my* actions. No matter what was happening, I was responsible for me—before God and my little girl. This knowledge kept me in check. It certainly inhibited me from reacting in response to the waves of feelings that rose up within me. It took every ounce of self-control I could muster to hold them all back at times, but if I were to be completely honest, which I am to a fault, I would have to say the knowledge of having *something* to control was actually quite empowering. This gave me a focus and a bit of determination, especially since it would have been so easy to let myself go everywhere at once.

The week prior to packing, I brought my daughter to Pennsylvania to run a women's conference I have been a part of for over ten years. Yes, somehow in my brokenness, God enabled me to carry on and manage my team and the guest speakers with strength and grace, even in harrowing circumstances.

But God.

For anyone who's ever experienced such pain and betrayal can attest, there are many emotions that are felt, sometimes all at once. Many of these were new for me to experience, and navigating them and the correlating thoughts can be a full-time job mentally. I will not go into great detail of the many thoughts that crossed my mind, but some were so intense, I felt I needed to speak them out to diminish their power and keep me accountable. I am grateful to report I did not act on one. Otherwise, my name could've easily become part of a news headline, and I'd be writing this in the comfort of an orange jumpsuit.

Knowing I was preparing to pack up my house the following week, I borrowed some large coolers from my parents' church. I planned to use them to pack up the freezer full of food I had in our basement, and I took them home with me to Ohio after the conference. These two long, white coolers were used by the church for their annual church family picnics. Because of their great length and size, they are referred to as "coffin coolers." Yes, this still makes me chuckle.

I left Tali at my parents' house in Pennsylvania and was now back at my home in Ohio to pack up, the two coffin coolers stacked on the back deck, ready to be filled. The next morning, my friend and neighbor Lori came over to see how I was doing and help me. I was having some negative thoughts involving the coffin coolers (in regards to my husband), and I wanted to confess to someone. As I greeted Lori at the back door, I pointed to the coolers and said with a smirk, "You see those coolers? They are called coffin coolers. I borrowed them to pack up my freezer, but I need you to make sure they are here each day until I leave and the freezer food gets packed in them—not anything else." She looked at me quizzically as my words didn't match the intensity to which my tone and facial expressions were implying. I'm pretty sure I was giving her a look somewhere between a wink and the stink eye, so I stated with renewed intensity, almost pleading, "Please make sure these are here each day. I need to know you will be checking on this." At first she chuckled, but when my countenance didn't lighten and I lowered my head and nodded, I could see understanding wash over her. So much was shared just with the exchange of glances. I was sure to tell every other woman who came through the back door that the coolers were there, and I needed help to pack up the freezer before I left. Many of them verbalized ideas for the coffin coolers, which were similar to my own, out of their own frustration and hurt. Honestly, it was refreshing to laugh off some of the anger that had been building. Oh, the blessings of friendship when walking through pain!

Thankfully, wisdom and the ability to push past my own emotions helped me to stay focused on what Natalia and I needed going forward, and I was able to determine the best next step. I decided to leave our home in Ohio and move into my parents' home in the Poconos. Since space would be limited with them, I took only what we absolutely needed and stored the rest in a family member's basement who lived nearby.

Depending on whether the items were going to storage or my parents', the box was placed either in my empty dining room or the sitting room in the front of my home. Boxes upon boxes were stacked in each room. I tried to stay mindful and take only what was needed for three months. For some reason, this number was stuck in my head, so I went with it. What did I absolutely need for three months? Sorting through a house full of stuff, it amazed me to realize what I actually 'needed' to survive. Even with this in mind, my perception was still skewed and I took with me *way* more than what was necessary, but it was comforting to know I had it, just in case.

Packing and moving can be stressful, even in the best of circumstances. I felt as though I was evacuating the devastation of my life and realized I would be taking my broken heart with me wherever I went from now on. It was completely overwhelming and unnerving. I wanted desperately to leave it behind: boxes piled everywhere, people touching and moving all of my belongings, not knowing or having a grasp on where anything is should I need it in the future. I kept crying out to God, "Please help me!!" These were often the only words I could utter, "Please, please help!" I was looking for Him. The weight on my chest kept the concept of peace so far from my reality. My skin literally felt as though it was peeling off my body as every nerve was on high alert. I couldn't feel Him. I couldn't see Him in this mess. It was too ugly for Him to have any part of it, and I had nothing to give me hope of a future. *How could a good God allow me to experience such heartache? How would I survive? How would I manage alone? How would I care for myself and my child?*

As quickly as all these questions cycled through my brain, they went unanswered. I knew I needed to keep making decisions for the moment I was in and could not think beyond it. In every sense, I felt truly helpless and hopeless for my future.

One morning during the week of packing, my friend, Melissa, came by to help. She provided food for everyone and set it up in the kitchen. At one point, she pulled me aside and showed me a beautiful decorative box with metal handles on the sides and a lid that lifts off the top. The word *FAITH* was written in fancy print, and the details in the design made it a decorative piece all on its own. I currently have it set up in my living room as part of the decor.

Seeing the word *FAITH* caused a tightening in my chest as I questioned whether I had any at the moment. I remember simply commenting on the beauty of the box thinking that was all there was to it. She had to open it for me to reveal its contents and explain what was in there. The worship team and choir I had worked with and been a part of for four years had quickly gathered a pile of gift cards for us, some for food or grocery stores, gas or clothing, and even ones in large dollar amounts that could be used anywhere. Hundreds of dollars in provision.

I don't remember my reaction. I do remember not feeling as though I could emit any emotional response toward anything, and therefore, my guess would be that I remained pretty flat and unresponsive. Looking back on it now and realizing how much of a blessing that generosity truly was, tears come to my eyes. I'm overwhelmed with gratitude toward all the precious people who have stepped in at various times, allowing God to use them to speak to my heart and encourage me in ways they may never know.

It's those moments, when we feel small and insignificant and lost, that God steps in and reveals that He sees us and He's right there with us. He has proven Himself faithful to me in times when I struggled to see Him or His goodness in my confusion and darkness. Sometimes, we may feel boxed in by our surroundings, as I physically did in my home at that time, trying to sort through and compartmentalize our lives and make sense of it all. We may struggle to make plans or move through our mess without any hope of a future. As we look to God for grace and choose to honor Him with our actions, He proves Himself faithful in our faithfulness. That's when we are handed a little box of faith.

3

The Debacle.

A s my life was coming undone, I began to refer to the whole situation as "The Debacle." It just seemed to work, and it was a more fitting term to use than any of the more colorful words that would often come to mind. I had been using the term for more than a month before I ever looked it up to be sure I was using it properly. After all, I do appreciate proper word choices and using words by their appropriate meaning. Even naming my daughter took great thought into the meaning behind it.

Debacle *(n): a great disaster or complete failure*[1]

Other meanings to the definition are fiasco, violent disruption, a breakup, or dispersion. In a military scenario, it can refer to a rapid retreat from a surprise attack. In reviewing the definition, I knew I had chosen the perfect word to describe the situation, so it stuck.

After dropping my daughter off at my parents' house in Pennsylvania, I was traveling the umpteen miles across Route 80

West with a broken heart and the task of packing up my Ohio home before me. I was still praying, pleading with God to work miracles in my marriage and processing all of the anger, pain, fear, grief and oh, so many more emotions along the way. Six hours alone in my vehicle, just me and Jesus. It was time to get some things off my chest.

I am fully aware that God hears our silent prayers, and I can personally attest to this. Sometimes, in order to be truly open, raw and real, we must yell our prayers and express our deepest anguish to Him. I also know He can handle it. He created the emotions that rise up within us, and He is the perfect outlet to process them with.

There I was, flying like a torpedo just launched, making my way across the long stretch of highway in my 2000 GMC Yukon XL. That vehicle was a beast, and the ride was smooth. Better yet, my screamed prayers echoed fantastically on the windows, and my music could be blared without being a nuisance to anyone. I was free to express and release all of the awfulness accumulated within.

It started with a few tears that turned into light sobs as I thought about the ramifications and reality of what I'd be facing at home. My husband wanted to meet at the house that night to go through financial paperwork and remove anything of importance to him. He wanted to divide our assets, take what was his and go, *but it was OURS!* At this point I felt his heart had completely hardened toward my daughter and me; he was cutting us out of his life. It seemed as if everything we worked to build together had lost its value to him.

Quickly, those light sobs turned into wailing, and waves of grief rolled out of the pit of my gut. God was getting an earful as I released my thoughts and anguish to Him. I was truly in my own zone that November morning and was oblivious to my speed or the cop that had been waiting for me to fly by.

The flashing of blue and red lights was a sobering punch back to the present, but the ache in my chest and the bleeding of my heart could not be stopped, even as the police officer approached the passenger side of my vehicle. I was able to pull over and even remembered to put my hazard lights on, but I could not stop the flow of tears.

The pleasant, middle aged man who approached my car with a gentle smile and kindly asked, "Where are you going in such a hurry?" was clearly not prepared for the emotional dumping he was about to receive. He had a slight forewarning as he looked up from his clipboard to see my blotchy-red forehead and tear-stained cheeks. Though I had sunglasses on, it was apparent that my grief was visible around them, and his expression quickly turned to compassion as I began to answer his loaded question.

"You see, sir, my husband and I have been married for almost ten years. He just revealed he has been having an affair and is leaving me. I just left my daughter with my parents in the Poconos, and I'm going home to pack up my house and move in with my parents in Pennsylvania." My bottom lip began to quiver and I could not stop the tears that were streaming down my cheeks, nor did I have the energy or strength to wipe them before they fell to my lap. "I'm so sorry, sir. I didn't mean to be going so fast. I'm just trying to get to my house in Ohio."

Compassion. The look on his face said it all. The tears welling up in his eyes let me know he truly heard me. I needed that. After he explained that I had been going 25 mph over the speed limit, he winked and said my brake light was out and needed to be fixed. The citation was written up for only the broken light, and by filing some paperwork within ten days, I would not receive a fine. He reviewed the steps I needed to take several times as he could see my emotional state might skew my memory. He wanted to be sure this didn't become a bigger issue as he apologized for even pulling me over and giving me something more to do or think about. He said multiple times, "Please be careful." His tone and expression was that of a father who clearly had a daughter and he treated me from that perspective.

Grace. I didn't deserve it. I was incredibly guilty of speeding and was truly aware of my wrong, but there it was, handed to me on the side of the highway while semi-trucks and other vehicles whizzed past. I needed it. Oh, how I needed that pardon. How I longed to tell my story and have someone validate the weight of the words and respond. Drive by therapy. The absurdity of an officer apologizing for pulling me over when I was obviously wrong and deserving of a ticket. The irony was enough to put an ever-so-slight smile on my face, even if just for a moment. A notable weight lifted after pouring out my heart to a stranger.

Relief. In those small moments, I was simply grateful to take a deep breath. The heaviness, an odd compression on my chest that hadn't lifted since I was told I was no longer loved, had eased up slightly. I reminded myself to breathe.

Somehow, I was learning lessons even as I grieved and processed anger. Even I, the one who had worked hard my entire life to do the right thing, needed grace. Though my mistakes didn't always negatively affect those around me, if left undetected or corrected, they easily could be my own undoing. The way the officer looked at me and responded was like a father. It was as though he was looking at his own daughter and trying to find words to offer support and hope while correcting me and encouraging me to remain safe. He could see my pain and knew I needed compassion, but he also knew that I needed to change my speed to remain safe.

It's the kindness of God that leads us to repentance. He sees our situations. He understands the reasons behind our actions and responses, but He is always gently correcting us and leading us to do it in a better way. He wants so much more for us than what we think is good. I'm incredibly grateful for the grace of God in my life and that I could see it in that moment. I leaned into it and embraced it. I heeded that correction and allowed Him to point out areas which needed redirection or change. By allowing Him access to our broken pieces, He is able to reshape us and rebuild us in a way that reveals His handiwork and craftsmanship.

The times I tried to clean up my messes or worked painfully hard to get something to work out, I botched it up and got frustrated with my imperfections and shortcomings. I wasn't able to get it just right or make it look the way I thought it should. My perfectionism was constantly getting the best of me. There were even times when I thought I could do it better than God. OUCH! How's that for brutal honesty? Just typing out those honest words is painful for this woman who has become so dependent on God and is *so aware* of my constant need for Him. My need for grace is astounding. It wasn't until I realized it was all too messy for me to fix that I was able to relinquish my control. For so long, I thought it was my battle to fight. I walked around with my fists closed, ready to throw down. I didn't give Him the chance to step in and move things for me. I didn't allow Him the room He needed to adjust the circumstances or lead me in the right direction. I knew this had to change. By letting Him in, I found grace. Grace for all of it. Grace to lead me away from my shortcomings and mistakes. Grace to understand He has a better plan. Grace for myself and for others. Letting Him take over has been the most freeing and life-giving decision I have made. He sees it all and knows better than me, and I now have the grace I need to trust Him.

4

All I Want for Christmas...

We got all of our necessities moved into my parents' the week before Thanksgiving of 2012. My brother and his family made the trek up from North Carolina and my sister and her family came from Lancaster, PA to spend the holiday with us. They came to support and do their best to distract us. A few times, I caught Tali laughing and playing with her cousins, and my heart ached a little less. I even let out a few laughs with my sister and sister-in-law. I realized that nothing or no one could take my joy or happiness unless I let them. I could still have happy moments in the midst of such grief. Days would come when I would smile a little longer and laugh a little louder. Not then, but someday.

As the kids were making their Christmas lists and talking about what they wanted, my head ached to think about pulling together a happy or even somewhat good Christmas for my daughter. I had nothing to celebrate. Especially the birth of a Savior who I felt wasn't doing anything to rescue me out of this hellish pit. He wasn't relieving the burning ache in my chest, and he wasn't doing anything to restore my marriage as I prayed. What was there to celebrate? My life was in shambles. I was living with my parents. I was holding my sobbing baby girl each night as she cried herself to sleep. There was nothing to rejoice about.

Tali made an extensive list that year. Many items would've been difficult to provide even when there had been two incomes. With none, well, I was experiencing a bit of anxiety. I badly wanted to assure her that, although life felt like death at the time, and everything she knew was stripped from her, she would not lack anything. Within reason, of course.

At the top of her Christmas list was that her daddy's heart would change and he would come home. Oh, the stabbing pain that pierced through my heart when I read those words. Even if I had all the money in the world, I couldn't buy her that one.

The next big thing on her list was a Barbie Dream House. I looked into the pricing of this item and was overwhelmed. The other items on her list were much less expensive but certainly didn't hold the excitement or long-term entertainment value like the dollhouse.

My parents and siblings each committed to buying something from her list, and I was grateful to check off a few items I knew she would be excited about. Silently, I prayed that God would "overload us with blessings" that year so I could afford to get her many of the other things she desired. Deep down, I longed to be able to get her everything on her list.

I know this may seem quite materialistic and shallow. I've wrestled with this at times as I've uttered prayers for my child's toys or things that would make my life more convenient. I've also known loss and grief and heartache and the inability to feel God and sense His presence in my life. We desperately needed to be able to see Him and His hand in our lives, and know that He heard our prayers and would answer them. We had lost faith in man, but we still needed to rebuild trust in our God.

As the family left after the holiday, I knew I had a few short weeks to pull together Christmas for my kiddo. There were a few things I needed to organize and manage from our move that I had set aside to regroup and enjoy family time. I had always been the one to pay the bills, so taking care of the finances was nothing new for me to learn and for this, I'm grateful. However, I struggled to find the mental energy it took to organize and process. I was working to transfer Tali's school records to a different state, open a new bank account, change over and forward mail—all normal things that need to take place when you move. But oh, how exhausting it was to think it through and make it happen all by myself. Each time I made a phone call to another company or organization, they asked what the purpose was for the change or the move, and I had to explain my current devastation. Though it was an opportunity to vent and potentially receive some sympathy, it was tiresome to repeat.

After all the bills were paid and everything was up-to-date (thanks to the gift cards that worked like debit cards), I was able to sort through what our monthly finances and needs would look like for the time being. As winter was in full swing, and I was in desperate need of a winter coat, I knew I needed to make that purchase a priority. There were also a few things Tali needed on the list, and I started itemizing them according to level of necessity.

With my box of faith set on the bed, I pulled out the gift cards and sorted them by category. Gas cards placed in one pile, grocery cards in another, department stores, etc. I was so excited to find a gift card in there to Kohl's with enough money on it to buy that much-needed winter coat. I let out a sigh of relief because one need would be specifically met without having to pull from any cash flow. I had received some Christmas cards in the mail by that time and set them in the box until I could handle sorting through them. I needed to be in a good place mentally to see everyone else's smiling faces and happy families. To my surprise, many friends and family sent gift cards designated specifically for "Tali's Christmas." Those cards started another pile, and I was determined to use them just for her.

The provision was coming in and I was seeing it. By grouping the gift cards all together, I was able to afford many of the items on her wish list.

I searched the stores I had gift cards for to see if any sold the particular Doll House she wanted, and was shocked to find one store had it on sale AND I had enough gift cards to cover the cost. My mom watched Tali and let me sneak out to do some Christmas shopping. As I went to the different stores and searched for the items on her list, I was elated to be able to check off every single item she asked for!

I needed this miracle. That's truly what it was. Tali needed it as well. Her understanding of me not working, and her dad no longer being present had already sparked questions about how we were going to survive on our own. Living with my parents was certainly a buffer and provided assurance of a home, but she was inquisitive and already asked about our ability to purchase food, pay for our car, phone, clothes, and whatever else she could think of that we needed. She even said, "Mommy, it's okay if you can't get me anything for Christmas. I understand." It's those moments, as a parent, that you choke back sobs and refrain from wanting to lavish anything they've ever asked for on them. I desperately wanted to prove it was all going to be ok. To reassure her we would have what we needed, and no matter what fell apart around us, we would never have to miss out or experience less. I knew this was wishful thinking and not the reality for most. For this Christmas, a miracle unfolded, and she would be able to see it with her own eyes when she opened her gifts.

Not only was I able to purchase the items she requested, but along with the steady stream of checks and gift cards came other presents from friends and family. Because of their generosity, Tali had clothes and other items to open, besides the gifts from her wish list. Of course, there was also the beautiful little white cabinet for her dolls and the clothes inside it I wrapped for her to open. As I placed all the gifts by the tree, I couldn't help but be amazed by the overwhelming blessings and provision that had come our way to redeem Christmas for us.

There God was. Though our hearts were broken, our lives were shaken, and we didn't know what was to come, we could see where God had stepped in and made an appearance. He was there. Right in the middle of our mess.

It's easy to lose sight of Him and His goodness. Our world can cloud our view of His blessings and provisions. Caught up in a whirlwind of trauma, grief, or even busyness, we can miss out on the outpouring of His love and doses of grace. He is faithful. He is true. He is with us through every season and phase of life. We just need to have our eyes open to look for Him. We need to train ourselves to pay attention. We can get so focused on the problem or what's lacking that we fail to see the solution or the provision. We need to look up from our mess to see the hand of the Father outstretched and ready to help (if we let Him).

5

It is Well.

We made it through Christmas with grief weighing heavy on our shoulders and tangible blessings set before us. We walked around with a mixture of emotions ready to surface at any given moment. There was gratitude despite the losses and hope in spite of chaos and pain. As we approached the New Year, we looked forward to a fresh start. All things new. We just wanted to wake up and feel peace in our hearts and joy as we stepped forward.

The morning of New Year's Eve, Tali and I were rushing around to pack an overnight bag so we could ring in the New Year with my sister, who lived two hours away. I also had to stop at a store on the way to her house and needed to get there before it closed for the day.

I went into my parents' basement to be sure our cat and bunny were fed and cared for before we left, and my mom came with me so that I could give her instructions about both. As soon as we approached the bunny cage, we knew something was wrong. Tali's bunny, Daisy, was lying on its side and was stiff. Instantly, I began to sob. "I can't tell her," I said to my mom. "I can't tell her. This is not right. Tali doesn't need this right now." My mom tried to hold me together in her embrace while everything around me was falling apart.

She let me know she would take care of the bunny while I went to tell Tali to keep her from coming downstairs and seeing her dead. As I was coming upstairs, Tali was trying to get around me to go down to say goodbye to Daisy before we left. I had to catch her and tell her not to go down. When she asked why, tears welled up in my eyes, and I could tell she was starting to figure it out. I said, "Daisy isn't alive any more. She must've been sick."

Tali dropped to her knees on the kitchen floor and wailed like I've never seen her do before. I sat down on the floor next to her and held her as we both sobbed. I didn't have any good answers for her. I didn't know what happened or why God allowed it. I was searching for those answers myself. My heart hurt for her. So much loss. So much heartache. When would it end?

I wanted nothing more than to see 2012 end. As we watched the New Year's celebration in New York City on the TV at my sister's, we sat there numbly hoping the next year would be better and we wouldn't lose anything more.

My mom had placed Daisy in a little box and set it outside to preserve her body in the cold Pennsylvania air while we were gone. Tali began planning a proper burial service and designated my dad, a minister for over forty years, to officiate. Though she was only seven years old, Tali planned a well-organized memorial service and reception. I had brought my nieces home with us so they could participate, and Tali invited her closest friend in the area to attend. Some sweet friends who worked with my parents at their church also made an effort to be there on that cold, snowy, January afternoon.

My dad and one of the staff pastors from the church he was pastoring had dug a hole in the woods of the property and placed a cross made of sticks at the grave site. My mom had wrapped the bunny box in daisy printed wrapping paper Tali had picked out and placed the box in the hole. Tali had also picked out a multi-colored daisy floral bouquet and gave each attendee a daisy to hold during the service.

Tali had requested that my mom read a poem. My mom found the most beautifully suited one for the occasion. Tali also wrote out the order of service and gave it to her Papa to follow:

1. Open in prayer and scripture

2. Nana reads poem

3. Tali shares a few words about her bunny and gives others a chance to do the same

4. Papa shares some closing words

5. We sing a song together

The song. Still today, years later, the words of that song choice run through my veins and is my theme for everything I have and will ever walk through. While I rocked Tali as a baby, I would sing it over her. Then, as I tucked her into bed each night as a toddler it always made the song request list: "All the Little Children of the World," "Yes, Jesus Loves Me," with a grand finale duet of "It is Well," which Tali affectionately referred to as "Peein' Like a River." She didn't know the real names and called the songs by the words in them, which, obviously, she couldn't pronounce. It always made me smile.

Every night, for several years, we would sing "our song," as she eventually began to call it. Many of the days we ended in this song were filled with blessing and joy. But woven in between were many that had been clouded by grief, heartache, and struggles for me.

When I sing this song, it always takes me back to just after

Natalia was born. By the time she turned one year old, I knew something wasn't right with my body and it's healing and functioning after giving birth. This was when I discovered I wasn't able to carry any more of my own children, and I needed to have the first of what turned into many major surgeries. But at the end of each day, I sang. Often through tears, I sang. Through grief and loss, I sang. While in physical pain, I sang. When we attempted to adopt and failed five times, I sang.

When peace, like a river, attendeth my way,
When sorrows like sea billows roll;
Whatever my lot, Thou hast taught me to say,
It is well, it is well with my soul.

It is well
with my soul,
It is well,
it is well with my soul.
-Horatio Spafford[2]

It is well. Somewhere inside of Tali's little heart, she knew of a peace that would run, like a river, through the pain and heartache that had muddied her soul. As I started to lead the song during Daisy's memorial service, tears began to flow from my eyes, and I sang through stifled sobs. One simple glance at me from my mom and then our sweet friends, and they, too, were singing through tears of the grief they felt for us.

Tali had distributed tissues as everyone arrived at the service, and they were now much appreciated and put to use. After we ended the song, our officiant, Papa, instructed us (per Tali's request) to each toss our daisy into the open grave as a symbol of saying goodbye. More emotions flooded to the surface, and I took this moment to grieve all that was dying in my life at that time.

Tali was the last to drop her daisy and say her goodbyes. We all stood behind her and waited as she did. Her sweet little friend stayed by her side. After Tali dropped her flower onto the box, her friend gently put her arm around her shoulders and didn't say a word to Tali in that moment. She just stood there and allowed her to take time to process. All the adults whispered, "Aw, that's so sweet," but for me, this simple gesture was used by God to speak life into my soul.

"That's me." I felt those words echo inside of me. I knew God was likening Himself to Tali's friend. Silent, but present. I had begged for God to shout louder than the noise of the chaos and grief. I wanted Him to yell at it all and command it to leave immediately. I longed for everything in my life to be instantly put back together and healed at His spoken word. The anguish of sin in this world is overwhelming, and none of us are exempt of the pain. Sickness, loss, abandonment, rejection, heartache—sin has ushered them all in. BUT in the midst of it all, God is near. Without experiencing so much grief and loss, I would never have known so much comfort and peace. As I watched my baby girl and her sweet friend, I was being reminded of the nearness of God in our sorrows.

> *The Lord is close to the BROKENHEARTED;*
> *He rescues those whose spirits are crushed.*
> (Psalm 34:18, emphasis added)

Sometimes He just gives us room to grieve. He lets us cry it out and share what feels broken inside our hearts. It's almost as if we need to empty out all the pain and grief before God can fill us with comfort and hope for tomorrow. This process comes in waves. Empty the grief, fill with hope, repeat. We do this over and over until we find a new normal and we are able to find new purpose and live out the promise of what is before us.

Grief is necessary for processing any loss. We can't run away from it. Believe me, I've tried and it caught up with me eventually. It's like a cloud that lingers over us until we acknowledge it, take it apart piece by piece, and give God room to heal every area in us that is broken. We can't tackle the whole thing at once; it's too much for our little hearts. But we can be intentional to bring each emotion and thought back to God as we move in the direction of healing.

I'm able to gauge if I've fully healed from things emotionally by my "triggers." These are different for everyone. A simple song, news or magazine article, commercial, or scene from a movie makes me realize there are still things I need to overcome. There are still dark clouds of pain and emotion hovering over me that I've failed to look at. Sometimes, even a sentence spoken by a friend touches on a sensitive area in my heart that requires attention and healing. These "triggers" cause me to feel the same way I did when the trauma originally occurred and remind me of that incident. If I don't recognize them for what they are and allow God to heal the deeper wound, I react to them as though they are a new offense. We get to decide how we respond in those moments. We can bite back in hopes to attack the pain we feel, or we can choose to address the issue. If we continue to react to the pain, we may end up attacking those who are there to love and support us through our healing.

With the gentle reminder that God was standing right there beside me, I realized I could turn to Him whenever I was "triggered." I developed a healthy habit right at the beginning of my grieving process that has been strategic in my growth and healing. As soon as the cloud of grief and pain caught up with me, I immediately took some time to talk to God about it. My prayers often consisted of, *"Lord, I don't understand why, but this really hurts."* Depending on what emotions are provoked, it may be important to wait until you are able to set aside a quiet time with just you and God. Recognizing what brings it on is also key to working toward your healing. Take back the power from your "trigger" by identifying it and not allowing it to overwhelm you with emotions that will rule your day. Learn to see them for what they are: reminders of pain that still need to heal.

Taking each of our hurts back to God invites Him to look at the pain with us and gives Him the opportunity to do the healing. Knowing we don't have to face it alone lifts a heavy burden we may feel. Seeing where He is, beside us, in the midst of it all, provides the comfort and peace we need to be able to say, *"It is well."*

6

Running on Empty.

I felt stuck in a thick fog of emotions I kept trying to push past just to function. I kept waiting, hoping it would lift and I'd have my mental clarity back, but it remained, hovering over my mind.

In spite of this, I was somehow able to make decisions when needed, often in moments of great stress and imminence. I genuinely felt the steady presence of the Holy Spirit guiding me every step of the way. At the time, I did not feel clever, nor was I clear-minded, so I simply remained obedient to listen and obey those little nudges as they came along.

One of those first promptings was both Tali and I would need counseling—this realization was crystal clear even in the midst of chaos. Considering the trauma and significant loss that Tali and I were experiencing, I couldn't disagree, but finding a quality Christian counselor for children is no easy feat, especially in the area where my parents were living. In calling around, I discovered the going rate was about $85 per session for one person. In light of this, I opted to only go every other week so Tali could attend weekly. Even still, the monthly cost for us both to receive counseling was $510. OUCH!! This was a hard financial pill to swallow, when I had no steady income to speak of. Adding to this financial stab, I had to drive an hour and a half each week to South Philly to get the *really* good counselors.

Each week, we would take the opportunity to stay with friends who lived halfway between home and the counselor. If it was an early appointment, it would help buffer the time we'd need to get up in the morning. When it was an afternoon appointment, it gave us a place to crash without driving the entire way home during the dinner hour. These friends were a Godsend to us during this time. They received us where we were at—messy and broken. They let me vent. I was raw and ugly and they loved me anyway. They saw my hurt and gave me a safe place to grieve. I am so grateful for their place in my life and their encouragement to keep pressing forward.

One particular week, I had a dentist appointment scheduled for the day after counseling, and my friend offered to watch my daughter as the dentist was only 20 minutes from them. It was much easier than driving all the way home and having to secure childcare before heading back to the appointment (as children weren't allowed at this particular office).

As we were arriving at counseling on Tuesday afternoon, my car's gas light went on. I knew I had exactly $100 in my bank account and $85 of it was going to be immediately debited at the counselor's. I noticed those transactions went through *so FAST!!!* There was no "pending" period for the money to be withdrawn and not much of a buffer to make a gas purchase.

That left me with $15 for gas that was supposed to take me 45 minutes to my friends' house, where we would stay overnight, and then another 40 minutes round trip to the dentist the next day and another 45 minutes of drive time to get home. It didn't add up! Another important detail to note is my SUV wasn't exactly kind to my gas budget, and gas prices at the time were around $3 per gallon.

God had been showing me He was RIGHT there in little ways

throughout my journey, and because I had seen His faithfulness before, I just knew He had this one. Though I can't lie, I was slightly nervous as I put all $15 in the tank as we left the counselor's and headed to my friend's house.

The next day, as I was arriving at the dentist, the gas light went on again. I sat at a red light and prayed, "Lord, please let me find enough change in my purse to purchase at least one gallon of gas to get me back to my friend's and then I can ask her for money, though I REALLY don't want to have to do that!"

I felt as though I had been humbled enough. I was abandoned and rejected by the one I had vowed to love until I died, I was living with my parents and carting my kid to counseling I couldn't afford, and to top it off, I was in need of a root canal. I had already asked so much of my friend to stay in her home each week as we traveled back and forth, and I certainly didn't want to ask her for money, too. Though she would've given it to me in a heartbeat, it would've been embarrassing to ask, even if just for a loan.

I knew I had a one dollar bill in my wallet and I was rifling for change that would hopefully add up. I prayed that maybe I'd find even one more dollar in there.

As I was sifting through receipts I had shoved in my wallet, I saw another dollar folded in half and wedged in among them. The tightness in my chest relaxed a bit as I realized I had almost three dollars to put toward a gallon of gas. As I separated the bill from the receipts and pulled it out, it took me a moment to process the numbers I was seeing on it. They were two numbers I rarely saw together on any cash I carried. I blinked a couple times, unfolded it, and then it hit me. It was a crisp, fifty-dollar bill! I don't know how anyone else operates when they lose everything and are scraping the barrel just to get by, but I'd imagine they'd typically hold on tightly to every morsel and could account for every penny as they are suddenly more valuable than ever. Simply put: when you're dirt poor, you don't misplace a fifty-dollar bill.

I look back on that moment with assurance God was and is with me. I could see Him. I was holding His provision in my hand. I used it to fill my tank with gas and had a few dollars to spare. Even though my heart hurt. Even though I was paying the price for trauma I didn't cause and certainly didn't deserve. Even though I was confused and broken, I could see God. Quite honestly, had I not been in such a desperate place emotionally and financially, I never would have had the opportunity to experience such miracles. I hated the trade-off at the time, but I can now see the blessings.

As difficult as life can often be, I have come to realize that without trials, we never get to see God reveal Himself in new and miraculous ways. Without experiencing a need, we don't have the opportunity to see Him provide. Without pain and grief, we would never know the depth of His healing and comfort. Without uncertainty, we would never understand His peace. Condition yourself to look to God as soon as a trial presents itself. Wait, with praise and anticipation, for what He is about to do. He will always show up.

7

Count Your Blessings.

After living with my parents for four and a half months, my daughter and I moved back into our old house in Ohio while all of our stuff still remained in storage. Our belongings were in three different houses in two different states. It was a season of life that was extremely difficult and heart wrenching, and yet I knew I was being obedient to God in the process. Though I still don't fully understand His reasoning for this step in my journey, He proved Himself faithful and provided grace to carry me through.

Shortly after arriving at my parents', I knew I would be going back to Ohio for a brief time. During my time staying with them, God was preparing my heart to go back to the very place it was broken. I was not looking forward to this, nor did I want to go back for any reason or circumstance. Even now, years later, it's painful to drive through the last town I lived where my family felt complete and so many memories were made together. I certainly wouldn't have made the choice to go back on my own, but the steady promptings of the Holy Spirit would not let up. The scriptures of confirmation and steps

I was led to take kept pointing me in that direction. Again, I felt like I was preparing for another three-month journey. This number seemed to resonate in my mind and was a small goal or timeframe for which to plan.

I thought at the very least, the purpose of going back would be to meet up with my divorce attorney in person and finalize everything quicker. I also thought my daughter would be able to see her father; four months had passed with only minimal contact.

I began preparing Tali for this transition, but wasn't really able to fill in the gaps of all the unknowns I didn't have answers to. I still didn't have a job and was surviving on an extremely small and limited income that comprised of mostly gift cards and others feeling "a prompting on their heart" to send a check here and there. Though I had no idea what finances would come in each month, I just paid each bill as it came, and somehow the provision was there for the next one. Most of the time, I was hanging on the edge of my seat waiting to see how God was going to provide for the next need like I was watching an incredibly suspenseful movie. It was, quite frequently, the day prior or day of the bill being owed that the provision would show up in the mail or was handed to me in passing.

Each envelope I opened typically included a little note that read, "I just felt it on my heart to send this." I recall one check having the word "OBEDIENCE" written in the memo section. I received this one about a year into my journey and I remember thinking, "Was this their act of obedience or a reward for mine?" I resolved it was both. As I took so many steps in the direction the Lord was leading, He continued to bless us and care for us. This was my cue to keep following those sometimes-strange promptings and keep moving forward.

Let me throw in a quick disclaimer. I wasn't perfect in all of it. I was simply obedient to follow the leading of the Holy Spirit in my life and I was rewarded in my faithfulness. I learned to truly trust the Lord, but it didn't come without testing or sacrifice or great pain. I messed up at times. I still do. I am human and imperfect like everyone is in this world. I made a promise to God as a teenager that no matter what, I would live for Him. There were many times in between I restated this pact for my own benefit as a reminder of the promise I made—almost like a renewal of a vow. When my health declined and I couldn't figure out what the cause was, I promised to live for Him. When I suffered a tear in an artery in my neck and faced a possible stroke and even death, I promised to live for Him. When adoption attempts failed over and over and money and the hope of growing a family was lost, I promised to live for Him. When I held babies in my arms that were promised to be mine and had to give them back, I promised to live for Him. There were so many times of testing in my life where I restated my commitment to serving the Lord—no matter what! This time was no different. My vow was still the same. I offered my broken, messy, bleeding self to Him and allowed Him to use me and my situation however He would (or could). I simply chose to keep looking to Him for direction and do my best with each day He gave me. Not perfect, just faithfully dependent on Him.

When we first arrived back at the Ohio house, I asked my daughter if it felt strange to be there without any furniture or familiar things. She amazed me by replying, "No. It's like camping except we've been here before." Her response in this moment allowed me to know that, because of my obedience to go back there for a season, God was providing the grace needed to carry her as well.

I was so afraid of damaging her more in the process of trying to find hope and healing. I didn't understand some of the things God was asking me to do and, quite honestly, I would advise anyone else against them. They weren't logical and I was acutely aware of this. However, I knew His voice, and I knew I needed to obey. As I took each nervous step forward, He was faithful to confirm that I was on the right path and dispelled my fears. Tali's responses to the steps I was taking were often the confirmation I was praying for, knowing she was okay with it. God didn't only give me the grace I needed for each step, but He gave her equal doses of grace to take those steps with me.

While staying in this empty shell of a house that held the faint memories of feeling like home, my daughter and I shared a full size mattress on a basic metal frame for our bed. We slept in her old bedroom with no curtains or blinds and no pictures on the walls. The rooms were empty. Our hearts felt equally empty, abandoned, and broken.

GRIEF.

Each night, we'd lie in bed with the moon visible through the window behind our heads, and I'd ask her what I could pray for before going to sleep. One particular night, she answered by saying there was nothing she needed me to pray for. How was it possible she had no needs? This was the neediest season of my life. What she didn't know is that I had to accept money from friends to keep the electric on in the house so we could have heat. We were able to eat and even eat out because one person consistently handed me gift cards to local restaurants. She had no idea that every time a friend invited us over for a meal, I breathed a sigh of relief because it was one less I was concerned about providing.

I told her, since she had no needs or requests, she should take a minute to tell God what she was thankful for. She began with, "Dear God, thank you for my mom and my warm bed, for this roof to cover us from the rain, a house to stay in, clothes to wear, our cats, my friends, my nana and papa, a car to get us around, food to eat, special places to visit, money to go to restaurants..." As she continued with her list of 20 things to be thankful for, I laid there in the dark with tears streaming down my face. She had no needs.

I was depleted financially and was equally depleted emotionally. I felt I had nothing left to offer her, but I was somehow able to instill in her a heart of gratitude. From that day on, we challenged each other to come up with five things we could be thankful for each day. We kept a journal of them and found ourselves recognizing the added blessings God was providing that we never would've noticed otherwise. Sometimes, it was as simple as coupons in the mail for things we needed to buy or getting to borrow videos from friends to watch a special movie. We often listed visits with friends or gift cards to restaurants. It wasn't always a major miracle but the little blessings each and every day that sustained us, taught us to be grateful, and see His provision.

One thing I've found to be incredibly difficult is seeing anything positive when daily doses of negativity are being dumped on you. It can feel like trying to find a needle in a haystack in the middle of a windstorm!

So after you have suffered a little while, He will restore,
support, and strengthen you, and He will place you
on a firm foundation.
(1 Peter 5:10b)

This verse kind of rubbed me the wrong way when I was in the middle of my storm. With no job, no financial support, raising a child who was suffering from emotional trauma and loss, trying to process the emotional trauma and loss as an adult, homeschooling, preparing for major surgery TWICE, navigating new friendships... well, let's just say I didn't exactly feel like I had been suffering a "little" while, and I certainly didn't feel strengthened and established!

There were times, I'll admit, I got swept up in the storm and felt hopeless and overwhelmed. But in those moments of brokenness, God consistently sent me what I call "Smiles from Heaven."

Going through a divorce is like experiencing a death. Malachi 2:16 states that God hates divorce, and that "to divorce your wife is to overwhelm her with cruelty." Other translations describe it as doing "violence to the one he should protect." When your heart has been wounded in this way, the recovery can be so treacherous to navigate. There are so many changes and losses you experience, and unexpected situations can cause you to feel like parts of your own heart are actually dying. This necrosis or death can easily spread, eat at you, and leave you lifeless if you don't fight it daily with the truth and hope only found in the Word of God. It's a wound that needs to be tended to and addressed regularly with a balm of truth to properly heal along the way.

When you've been abandoned or rejected by someone, despite how many people you still have rallying around you who love and care for you, it is easy to feel isolated, alone, and thrown away like a used take-out container. Forgive me for the poor imagery, but you get the idea that you feel worthless. Your value and purpose can be so hard to see. If someone could disregard you like they do trash, how easy it could be to believe this is what you are.

Not only did I need to remind *myself* of the truth of who I was in Christ, but I needed to be reminded by *Him*. 1 John 5:1 revealed to me I was a daughter of the Most High God and I was loved and cherished by Him. I heard this at church and from friends, but I needed to experience the care and attention from Him personally. He was so faithful to show me He was my provider and I would lack nothing, but I certainly didn't feel cherished or adored by anyone.

Everything around me felt like death. Though I was currently living in my old home, I knew I was going to lose it forever in the process of the divorce. I had already lost a life I loved and all I knew. Everything in me ached. I remember looking around our vacant and sparsely furnished home and the fleeting thought that fresh flowers would brighten it up passed through my mind. Something so simple would've been such a luxury and certainly something I couldn't afford at the time. As quickly as the thought came, I was able to rationalize it right out of my mind just the same. I wasn't buying flowers any time soon and I certainly didn't have anyone else in my life to do so. Next thought.

Our local grocery store had a membership program that would offer discounts each time I swiped my card when I made a purchase. It would also track my regular purchases and periodically send me coupons for items I bought most often. A few days after my thought about flowers came and went, I received another little booklet of coupons in the mail. With this set, I got the usual ones for things like yogurt, butter, and juice, which were oh so helpful. The difference, this time, was the coupon for a free bouquet of flowers from the floral department. Lord knows I had not been buying flowers! This was another one of those moments that I genuinely felt the care of my Heavenly Father. He saw me. He knew even the smallest desires of my heart, the ones not uttered to a single soul, and He met them so many times. Little and sometimes major blessings would come our way when I least expected it. As I started to trust God to step in and meet our needs, I recognized more and more the blessings He was providing along the way.

My focus became less on what I was lacking and more on what God was doing for me. The more I turned my attention to Him, the more I could see Him in my situation. I could trust Him! He was incredibly faithful to provide, and I was able to live worry free concerning where our next meal or rent check would be coming from. I knew we would have EXACTLY what we needed when we needed it. And we did!!

In my suffering, I learned to trust Him, PERFECTLY.

He CONFIRMED that I could, daily.

My trust was STRENGTHENED and I became deeply rooted and ESTABLISHED in Him.

I encourage you to take a step in the direction of seeing the blessings. Choose to see what IS good despite what is going on around you. Try to make a list of all you are grateful for in this moment. See if you can come up with 20 things today. Challenge yourself to come up with at least five things you can thank God for each day. If you struggle to see the blessings in your every day, this will help to shift your perspective from all that is lacking to all that you already have. You will notice so many "smiles from Heaven" that trickle into each day that we so often fail to see. Enjoy a new journey to gratefulness.

$\mathcal{8}$

The Debacle Continues.

I needed to see the consistent and evident blessings from God during this uncertain season to re-build and establish my trust in Him. I had to know, without a doubt, He was going to provide for us. This was even more important as I felt Him prompting me to move to Georgia.

As I mentioned before, a move, any move—to anywhere— no matter how exciting or positive, is stressful and comes with challenges. But when you feel as though you need to remind yourself to breathe in each moment of the day, any major decision beyond that is daunting.

I desperately needed steady provision. And so much GRACE.

There were many circumstances and details to my situation that would make a major move impossible. I was well aware of this... and so was everyone on this journey with me. I knew, in the deepest parts of my heart, our next step was Georgia. At the time, I couldn't perfectly articulate why, other than the fact that I knew the Holy Spirit was prompting me, and we needed a brand new place to start over.

We had been living on gift cards and wads of cash from dear friends who felt compelled to take money out of their wallets and press it into the palm of my hand. Tears would well up in both of our eyes and they would apologize for it being "all the cash they carried" or wishing it could be more. They understood my need without me saying a word. It was always just enough to get us over an immediate financial hurdle. The timing was impeccable. Always.

Moving away from my caring friends and family to a place where I only knew one couple seemed foolish. This was a time in my life when I needed all the support I could get, yet I felt a continuous nudging to step out into the unknown. I genuinely sensed God reminding me, over and over, "I am your provider."

In taking this step (or rather giant leap) of faith, I took a trip down to Georgia to search for apartments and a job; my friend, Amie, was gracious to host us during the process. Most apartment complexes, believe it or not, wanted you to be able to show you lived within the state and worked at your current job for a period of time. I had proof of neither. I also needed to verify I earned three times the rent in monthly income. Again, no proof. A landlord or rental agency doesn't respond well to "I'll be paying my rent with gift cards and checks that God instructs random people to send me." You can trust me on this one. I know.

Oh, and did I mention the need for first and last month's rent PLUS one month's rent for a deposit? This mama did not have that kind of extra cash on hand. We were living on "daily bread." Just as daily deliveries of manna were provided for the Israelites, we, too, know what it's like to get our needs met one day at a time. There was just enough provision for each day or moment.

After almost a week of spending the entirety of every day searching for jobs and housing, I had exhausted all possible leads. I had finally broken down and cried in front of my dear friend, Amie, and explained that I had literally looked everywhere and followed every lead that came my way. She offered to come with me the next day and help me in my search. Before we left, Amie received a phone call. She answered the phone and let the other person know what we were up to for the day and asked her to pray.

Coincidentally, the woman on the line worked for an elderly couple who was looking for a 'live-in' to help with some light cooking and shopping in exchange for room and board. Though this wasn't my first choice, I was willing to check it out if it meant getting us to Georgia.

When Amie and I met with the couple later that day, it finally seemed like pieces were falling into place. They had two large rooms with a private bath for us to stay in upstairs, as well as an attic area for storage. They offered to provide our housing, food and a few other perks if I prepared meals and drove them to various appointments.

During this initial visit, the older woman, a retired social worker, seemed sympathetic to our situation and our need for a place to find healing and rest. She told us to move in and take our time getting settled before we got started with a regular schedule of tasks in their home. I felt as though this was the open door we needed to get to Georgia and could easily handle the workload they were requesting. We set a date for move-in and got the plan in motion.

We hauled all our belongings to Georgia and got moved into the upstairs of our "new home." I explained to the couple it would take me about a week to get settled and sort through our belongings before I could jump into regular work mode. We were spending our nights at Amie's when we arrived, because I was waiting on a newly ordered mattress to be delivered. We went over to our new place each day and worked on getting things set up and organized, checking in with the couple to let them know where we were in our progress.

They had a few visits and shopping trips they wanted us to take them on that week, and we obliged. Though this wasn't what we had originally agreed upon or discussed, I was more than willing to accommodate the needs as I felt so blessed to be offered so much in exchange. And then the sofa arrived…

Along with my mattress, I ordered a new little sofa that fit perfectly in the room that would serve as our living room. Our two upstairs rooms were in complete disarray and each day I worked to get them organized enough for us to move in. Some of our items had been in storage or in boxes for almost a year and I packed them in such a flurry that I couldn't even remember what I had left or where it was. I was also in the process of getting Tali registered for school and digging through necessary paperwork to do so. It felt chaotic, and I was working tirelessly to try to establish some order and create a peaceful space. Amie volunteered to come over one evening to help get some things unpacked and put the sofa together (it was shipped in boxes). When we walked in the door of the house, the woman stood up from where she was sitting at the kitchen table and began screaming at us for not letting her know how long I would be gone and when I would return and something else about their dog going up the steps to my room and her not being physically able to retrieve him. We felt like teenagers being scolded for staying out after curfew. Except this wasn't our mom. This wasn't a woman I knew well at all. I was already hurt and broken, and this poured salt into a gaping, open wound. I was in shock.

The issue she had with me was nonsensical and I was struggling to figure out why it caused her to escalate to the level of screaming at the two of us. I was just grateful my child wasn't present for such an assault. My heart was grieved all over again, and I was so confused. How could this situation seem so perfect and then become a disaster? As Amie and I retreated to the upstairs to get the couch put together, I broke down, yet again, in front of my friend. She helped me to come up with a plan to address what happened with the couple the next day. Though I handled the situation with more grace than I possessed on my own, I was baffled and angry I had to deal with a confrontation over something so futile. I was also fearful it would happen again and my child would be subjected to her wrath, but I decided to give her a second chance and set clear boundaries. I made her aware that the way she addressed me was inappropriate, and I wouldn't tolerate any such behaviors around my child.

She complied, apologized, and recognized where she had jumped to conclusions, and also made promises to communicate her needs and expectations clearer. Tali and I officially moved in, and we established a cooking and shopping schedule for that week. I had cooked a few days and had Thursday "off" from any household duties. I continued to unpack for most of the morning and then promised to take Tali to the community pool that afternoon. We needed a break from boxes and could use a good dose of vitamin D. Our plan was to stay at the pool until late afternoon, and eat some leftovers for an early dinner so I could get back to unpacking some boxes. We were also preparing for a two-week trip to see family in Florida and I was trying to get packed for that as well.

When we left for the pool, the couple had already gone out for the day. We noticed they were back at home when we arrived around 4:00PM, but soon realized they were napping and did our best to be quiet as I heated our dinner. As I turned to grab something from the fridge, the woman appeared from around the corner. I never heard her approach, but there she was, standing in front of me, leaning on her cane with a disturbed look on her face. Her eyes were fierce, and it was obvious by her expression that she was perturbed. She kept her voice low and spoke angrily through clenched teeth as she said, "It is customary to invite the others in the household to have dinner with you." Again, I was in shock at her controlled display of anger. I was able to utter that I recognized they were sleeping and didn't want to wake them. I also managed to get out something else about us just coming back from the pool and getting an early dinner since we were hungry. I was suddenly trying to defend myself. As though she didn't hear a word I said, she clenched her teeth and contorted her face even more as she repeated her statement, slightly louder and with more emphasis on certain words, "It is *customary* to invite the others in the *household* to have *dinner* with you." Still in shock, I was able to manage an apology for being unaware of such a custom and I was raised to never disturb someone when they were resting. Then I offered, "But now that you are awake, you are welcome to join us. I don't mind heating something up for you." She huffed back in an annoyed tone, "Well, I don't really feel like eating somewhere I wasn't invited. We will just wait till you are finished here and eat on our own."

Seriously? Was this really happening? How did I get trapped in a beautiful home with an irate, nonsensical woman? I couldn't figure out how I ended up here. I was struggling to make sense of what was happening and how I had been unaware of such customs for so long. Was this a southern thing that we northern girls were ignorant of? Did I really have to learn a new set of "customs" to live in the south? How could I continue to live in a house where I had to play these mind games while trying to find rest and establish a new life with my daughter? Based on these two incidents and some other odd exchanges with the couple, where passive-aggressive behaviors were openly displayed, I knew that this wasn't a healthy environment for us to continue to live in.

It was incredibly difficult moving to Georgia and getting into this house. I worked hard to unpack and settle in, and I was overwhelmed at the thought of trying to move again. Aside from the fact that I still had no proof of steady income, I also had no crew of friends in the area to help me move again. The first group that came to help unload were from Amie's church and volunteered to get us moved in, but I doubted they would come to help a second time. Especially considering it hadn't even been a month.

AND I had nowhere to go! I was starting the housing and job search all over again. I knew that even if I was lucky enough to find an apartment that accommodated all my limitations, I still had no way to pay the monthly rent and utilities on my own. There were many times I broke down from the weight of carrying these heavy loads alone. I cried myself to sleep A LOT.

Each morning, I was forced to make a decision. Giving up was always an option. I bargained with God to make all the pain and struggle to survive magically disappear. I wanted peace, rest, and to feel like I could breathe again. For almost a year I felt this heaviness—a constriction in my chest. The aching in my heart wouldn't go away. The anger at the foolish choices of others who threw me into this terrible pit in the first place was ever-present. I wanted justice. I wanted to wake up from this never-ending nightmare. If I just stayed in bed, could I avoid all the pain and worry of the world? This was a tempting idea.

I brought all of these thoughts and feelings to God. Every day. Many times throughout my journey of healing, I talked it all out with Him. I had to constantly communicate with Him to know His thoughts and His ways and hear His wisdom for each moment. Before I stepped out of bed, while many worries flooded my mind, I invited Him to be a part of my day. To walk with me. To help me. I pleaded with Him often for peace and grace. Whenever I faced another decision, I turned to Him. Honestly, without making the daily choice to depend on Him, I wouldn't have survived. I looked to Him for strength and I found it. Every time.

Many times, I thought: *If I couldn't figure out a way to overcome, how would my daughter ever learn to?* I had to keep pushing through and fighting for her. She had to know what bravery in the face of adversity looked like. She had to see the rewards of obedience to God and the benefits of trusting Him. She had to observe total dependency on Him. I wanted to lie down and let the circumstances of life just run over me instead of continuously smacking me in the face. But I knew there was a greater purpose, and I needed to keep getting up and fighting each day.

Along with the daily encouragement I sought from the Word of God, there were a few mantras that replayed frequently in my mind. One of them was "Never, never, never give up." Sometimes we need reminders to help us continue to step forward and see what the next day holds. I kept reminding myself tomorrow would be better than today. I would replay these quotes in my mind throughout the day. I was also intentional to post scripture or encouraging quotes on the walls of whatever room I was sleeping in. I made sure they were visible from where I laid in my bed so before I fell asleep, when I was restless in the middle of the night, and before I stepped out of bed each morning, I was absorbing truth. When our lives seem uncertain, it's important to seek what is true and let this truth rest like a salve on our wounded soul.

When you go through deep waters, I will be with you.
When you go through rivers of difficulty, you will not drown.
When you pass through the fire of oppression,
you will not be burned up; the flames will not consume you.
(Isaiah 43:2)

Memories of painful moments would surface in my mind when I least expected it. Even months, sometimes years, after the initial trauma, my mind would take me back like I was reliving the moment all over again. It was clear I hadn't processed those hurts and moved toward healing. Each time this would happen, I had to offer them to God and ask Him to help me see where He was when I was being hurt. As I flooded my mind with the truth of His Word, I was able to see His presence was with me all along the way and His promises stood firm.

I recall sitting on the couch in my living room back in Ohio before the first move, with my little girl seated on my lap and my arms wrapped tightly around her. A sweet woman from our church, who Tali knew as "Gamma Wancy," sat in the chair opposite us. Abby's husband and the youth pastor from our church, who was also a dear friend of ours, was there too. They were there for support, to just be present with us as we hurt. While we sat there my now ex-husband was upstairs packing up his belongings to move out.

Earlier that morning, I held my baby girl in the same manner in the living room of my pastor's house while my ex-husband looked at my daughter and told her he was leaving us and moving out. I cannot begin to express the ache that overwhelmed my chest. I was hurting for myself and now for my little girl who was lost and confused. She had tried to wrap her mind around the words he spoke but couldn't figure out why a daddy who loved her would walk away. How could he tell her he would always love her, but was packing his things to leave her? In that moment, actions began to mean a lot more to her than words ever would.

I held her as tight as I could so she knew I was there and I wasn't letting go. Tears streamed down my face as she asked why he had to go and where was he going. Then, she made a statement that hit each of us in the chest and caused our friends to release the tears they had been desperately trying to hold in. "Mommy," she said quietly and somewhat matter-of-fact, "this is the worst day of my life." I affirmed I was feeling the same way. Trying to hold back sobs, I assured her that even though this was the worst day, every day from here on out would be a little bit better.

I was hopeful somehow we would heal from this initial blow to the heart and we would find a way to go on. I was equally confused. My mind was swirling with thoughts and fears of the unknown, but I knew in that moment, as I was holding my little girl so tightly, God was doing the same for me. I felt Him holding me close, assuring me He was right there. He wasn't going to leave me like others had. He wasn't going to get bored with me or fail to see my value one day. He was so intentional to let me know He was right there, every step of the way.

"If you are going to go through hell, keep going"—another mantra that came to mind during the throws of searching for an apartment in Georgia yet again. Since we had survived the worst day of our lives and God had sustained us in miraculous ways for ten months, I knew if I kept walking forward He would faithfully guide and take care of us. I stopped praying for God to pick me up and place me on a peaceful island in the middle of the ocean and instead prayed for Him to guide my steps.

Pain screams deafeningly loud. It's silent, but it has a way of clouding your thoughts and obscuring your vision. It's the loudest silence I've ever known. When things came up which required me to think logically or clearly, I needed to cling to God and His wisdom to avoid human error. I asked Him daily to help me hear His voice above the pain. It wasn't easy, so I needed to intentionally listen and trust He was faithful to direct my path.

"I will work as hard as I can to find the right place for us," I committed my part to God and followed with a request, "but I need you to intervene and lead us to the place that works with our financial situation." I called dozens of apartment complexes and narrowed our search down to about three or four that seemed willing to accept a co-signer and required a minimal deposit. We visited each one and by a natural process of eliminating the ones with roaches scurrying about or ones that seemed unsafe, we narrowed it down to one we could call "home" for a while.

By the time we got all our stuff moved in, I felt like I could breathe slightly deeper than before. It was our first place alone together that was just ours. We could start over and make a brand new life.

9

I am Your Provider.

We moved in at the end of August 2013. I worked tirelessly to get unpacked, start homeschooling as soon as possible, and develop some sort of normal schedule or routine. Our lives had been nomadic and each day had been unpredictable, so I hadn't planned ahead in a long time.

I used to be the queen of schedules and planning. I'd have days, even months, mapped out, but when my world tipped over I struggled to commit to a plan because I feared something would happen to disrupt it. I went from being the guru of preparing ahead to being one of those people who could only decide to do something within the present week. This was uncomfortable for me, but my life was uncertain and I was forced to get out of this cycle. Because I couldn't trust what tomorrow would hold, I learned to trust in the One who holds tomorrow.

Each day before I stepped out of bed, I prayed and asked God to be with me, help me get up, and work through the tasks ahead of me. I was emotionally and physically spent, in continuous need of doses of grace and strength.

Because we found ourselves in a place that required monthly rent, I felt I needed to find a job to support us. This entirely logical thought process prompted me to begin my search. I had a degree in nursing and was hopeful that something would be available which would allow me to potentially work from home or have a schedule that was flexible enough for me to get childcare for Tali and continue to homeschool her.

For many, it would be a no-brainer to put their child in public school so they could go back to work. I get it. It's logical. I too, struggled with this reasoning, but I didn't have peace about sending Tali to public school. Homeschooling was the one constant in my child's life. We moved to a new state, new apartment, and experienced many months of uncertainty and trauma. We needed rest, and we required time to heal. Sending her to school would've been another major adjustment. Let me say this: if I felt that was the way God was leading me, I would've embraced it in faith. But I didn't have peace about it at all. So I kept looking into other solutions for work. I'd make phone calls, follow leads, and end up nowhere. The position would be filled, or it would be crazy full-time hours or have a long commute. It wasn't coming together, and as the weeks passed I was getting frustrated and nervous as to how we'd pay our bills.

October rent was nearly due, and slowly money was trickling in from various sources as it had for months. More significant amounts of money were coming in, and we had what we needed to pay October's bills. After several weeks of not being able to find work, I knew it was time to apply for welfare. I had exhausted all other options and nothing was working out. Though this was a huge dig at my pride, I knew it was time to ask for help. God was faithful to provide, but I needed to do all I personally could to help my situation. I searched for the Georgia state welfare page and clicked on the button to apply for food stamps. When I did this, a new page opened up. The screen was all black except for white writing in the center of the page. It read, "Due to an error with our system, we are unable to accept any new applications for public assistance at this time." Any other time in my life, this would've thrown me off and caused me to lose hope. My normal response would've been to break down and cry. But because I had been conditioned to fully trust God for everything I needed, when this message popped up, I just sat back and smiled. I heard God whisper to me in that moment, "I am your provider."

I was able to hear His voice over the confusion of the moment and the uncertainty of tomorrow. I knew in the depths of my spirit He was still taking care of us and I could trust Him no matter what.

Throughout that month, I felt increasingly tired and experienced twinges of pain in my abdomen. I kept brushing it off, thinking I had simply exhausted myself from two moves and unpacking. We now lived in a second story apartment and were required to bring our trash to a centrally located dumpster on the property. We had to carry our laundry down the flight of stairs and take it to an on-site laundromat. I was merely thinking all of this extra lifting and carrying was causing me some muscle aches or pains.

By the end of the month, the pain became unbearable, and I ended up going to the emergency room. Something wasn't right. I felt I must've pulled a muscle or developed a hernia. I couldn't take the pain any longer and needed professional help.

Taking myself to the hospital and not having the person you always called to be with you in an emergency was incredibly unsettling. We required a new plan. We needed someone to fill the gap during this season of our lives.

Shortly after we moved into our apartment, I realized a childhood friend of mine was living only minutes away. I knew she was in Georgia and somewhere in our vicinity, but I had no idea how close she actually was until we were moved in and somewhat settled. She invited us over to her beautiful home at the base of Kennesaw Mountain, seated on many acres of farmland and overlooking a pond.

Instantly, she and I reconnected and hit it off after sixteen years of being apart and not having contact. Her home became our haven—a resting place from the stressors of the rest of the world. She and I would sip cups of hot tea and chat about the many new and old things in our lives. We both had been on some unique journeys and experienced God's grace. We could share our rough moments and find new things to laugh and smile about. She, with her husband and two kids, would invite us for dinner or afternoon picnics. They blessed us with a love and care I will forever cherish.

I was able to call my old/new friend, Crystal, and let her know I needed to go to the emergency room. I was able to drive, but my situation was worsening. I needed to have tests done immediately and not wait for a visit to be scheduled at a doctor's office. Without hesitation, she told me to drop Tali off on my way so I could get checked out without having to worry about her.

After hours of testing and waiting for answers, the results revealed I had a large mass on my left ovary that had grown to the size of an orange. I needed to follow up with a surgeon and have it removed as soon as possible. Sitting alone in the cold emergency room, connected to monitors and an I.V. pole, the severity of my current situation was slowly hitting me.

I cannot even begin to fully express the weight this wave of news heaped on me. For one, I was in physical pain and completely exhausted from my body fighting and attacking the mass. Secondly, I had recently moved to a different state with new friendships starting, and I struggled to not feel like the "needy new girl." I had always been the one to take care of others and help them out in difficult times. To be the one asking for help was uncomfortable and unnatural for me.

I hadn't even had the chance to establish a regular family doctor, and now I needed to find a surgeon. I tried asking some of the people at my new church (who I barely knew) for suggestions, but was not having any success. Because of an extensive surgery almost two years prior, I had to find someone knowledgeable of what had been done in the previous surgery in order to proceed with this one. The journey of my health issues is a whole other book yet to be written, but let me just say this: I have a genetic disorder called Ehlers-Danlos Syndrome that has wreaked havoc on my body and complicated my current issues immensely. My apprehension of the "white coat" was not helping either. Every time I finally went in to see a doctor, I was notified of many issues that were occurring and needed to be fixed or addressed.

Once again, I took my neediness to the Lord. This was another God-sized problem, and I needed more direction and another hefty dose of grace. I didn't know how I'd find a doctor or how I'd manage surgery on my own, but I knew God hadn't left me yet, and He had already made it clear He was invested in my cause. So forward we went.

Even though I walk through the darkest valley, I will fear no evil, for you are with me; your rod and your staff, they comfort me.
(Psalm 23:4, NIV)

I finally understood why I wasn't able to find a job. Had I begun to work, I would have to take off 8-10 weeks immediately to recover from surgery. I wouldn't be able to give full focus and attention toward healing, because I would push through my recovery and try to get back to work sooner than recommended. Ultimately, I would rely on my own ability to provide for us rather than waiting on God for his daily portions.

He consistently reminded me, in every opportunity possible, that HE was My Provider. *Jehovah Jireh.*

10

A Paper Dress.

I am sure I can speak on behalf of all women when I say our least favorite doctor visit is going to see the gynecologist. I had avoided going to the doctor, in general, throughout the last year of turmoil. Now I had to seek one out to get necessary help and one that could meet all my specific health requirements.

I told God exactly what I needed in a doctor (as if He didn't already know). Then, I proceeded to look online at reputable local hospitals and their list of doctors. I prayed the right one would be revealed to me, and I would somehow know who to call. I looked through countless photos and read their profiles. I narrowed down the list by their experience or an expression on their face that annoyed me. Some of them hadn't worked with the da Vinci Surgical System necessary for the procedure I needed, and that weeded them out immediately. It took time to filter through many candidates, but I kept coming back to one in particular.

She had a kind face. She also possessed the experience and expertise needed for my case. There was something that resonated within me, helping me to know this was "the one."

Dr. Caroline, as I will refer to her, was instrumental in helping me navigate the uncertainty of the surgical procedure. I remember how nervous I was being escorted into one room where a nurse took several tubes full of blood, checked my vitals and weight, then led me to a private exam room. I was instructed to put on the classic paper gown with nothing underneath, and as I sat on the exam table, my bare bum was exposed to the cold office air. I tried to cover up with the paper blanket provided, but to no avail.

I had been to enough doctors to know there were some good ones in a large pool of not-so-good ones. Every new patient appointment was unsettling to me because you just never know what you are going to get. There I was, in the most vulnerable situation imaginable, about to meet someone who would potentially hold my life in her hands. The surgery I faced was daunting. I felt abandoned, alone, and needy. My life was upside-down and messy, and I was about to meet a stranger wearing only a paper dress with my backside hanging out.

There was another issue that needed to be addressed that day which I had avoided for over a year. It had remained in the back of my mind, but with all the other trauma I had been experiencing, I couldn't face another thing. Since I had to be at this doctor's office anyway, it was time to bring it up.

As my ex-husband made his grand departure, he dropped an extra bomb on me that I never expected. Aside from the affair he was currently having, he also had multiple affairs throughout our marriage. I knew several of the women and was fully aware of their own promiscuous history. Thus, I felt it necessary to be tested for a wide gamut of venereal diseases. I wanted to be sure none of the physical discomforts I was currently experiencing were caused by something other than the mass that had been detected.

This was a hard reality for me to face. It caused astronomical anger and pain to rise within me. I had saved my body and my virginity for my husband. I valued this gift I could offer. I cherished the idea of having one companion for life and sharing myself with only that one person. What I valued, he did not. He treated my gift with such lack of care it was defiling. Here I was about to address the possibility of having some disease my actions didn't warrant. I don't bring this up for any shock value or plea for sympathy. It was an added layer to my emotional pain and increased my level of vulnerability and anxiety going into this appointment. After meeting many women who have walked through circumstances similar to mine, I've realized this is a common issue for people with unfaithful spouses. Too many have suffered the negative effects of their partner's actions. Until this became my own reality, I had never considered this when I heard stories of adulterous spouses.

While I was living with my parents, I read as much as I could about the effects of affairs on a marriage and healing from such wounds. Lucky for me, my dad had been a pastor for forty years, and he had just completed his master's in counseling, so he had a library full of reading material in his office. Several of the books I read through were written by well-known and reputable psychologists who had over twenty years' experience in this field. Each of them related that the emotional trauma a spouse endures when their partner has been unfaithful is like that of a rape victim. I learned the same process of healing is necessary and the emotional effects on the person are quite similar. Though I have not experienced both forms of trauma to draw my own comparison, I have heard and read testimonies of women who have experienced rape, and I can relate to the emotional and psychological damage endured.

I wanted to avoid the pain and layers of trauma I had experienced, but this visit to the doctor was forcing them to the surface and shoving them in my face. I had been in the mode of putting out one fire after another, trying to survive. Each one caused more pain for me to process, and it had been too overwhelming to wade through it all. Some of it was avoided or stuffed so I could manage the issue at hand and keep plowing forward. My physical issues were now the biggest fire to extinguish, and with them came emotions I wasn't wanting to address. However, I didn't really have a choice. Here I was.

When the doctor came in and introduced herself as Caroline, I immediately knew she was different. She asked me a few basic questions and the answers caused me to reveal I had recently moved into the area. She followed up with, "So what brought you to Georgia?" In that moment, I knew this was the place to unload. Her demeanor and gentle approach allowed me to feel safe, even though I was in an incredibly vulnerable position. As I told my story and began to sob, she got up from her little round stool and embraced me. She held me and let me weep as a trusted friend would. With air breezing through the back of my paper dress, I laid my head on this stranger's shoulders and cried out all the tension and pain I had been trying to hold in and keep together.

As we talked through the plan of care that lay ahead, she discussed each option as though she was my friend and guided me through the process of making the best possible decision for my health. She discussed all the tests she felt necessary to run based on my ex-husband's history and some of the other issues I was experiencing. I desperately needed a friend to hold my hand through all of this, and God gave me one in the form of a gynecologist.

I've found once I think I have everything in life figured out, I face a situation that reveals I know nothing about anything. The unknown used to rattle me; I needed to know everything so I could feel safe and in control. I slowly found freedom and blessing in "not knowing." This was the place God had room to do what only He could without me getting in the way. He has always been faithful to supply grace for the unknown. On that day, my grace came in the form of a doctor. For a person who had been jaded by medicine a time or two, I was a grateful recipient of such grace in this moment.

Aside from the growing mass in my abdomen that needed to

be dealt with quickly, all my other test results came back negative. I wasn't in need of any added treatment. 'Relief' does not adequately describe my feelings after hearing that news. The word doesn't seem powerful enough for the weight that was lifted off my chest. However, now that I didn't have any added physical issues to deal with, I had to navigate the emotional issues that were brought up relating to why I needed the tests in the first place. This was uncomfortable and painful territory.

Physical pain is an indicator of some form of trauma that has occurred or is occurring in our body. Emotional pain is the indicator of trauma we've endured or are currently experiencing. Both require attention and healing. If avoided, the issue will affect our everyday living and can even spread to cause worsening effects. Emotional pain or trauma not processed and healed can and will lead to anger, bitterness, and resentment. These are like the cancers of emotion; growing and infiltrating into every facet of your being.

We must be intentional about seeking treatment for both. I suppose God may choose to heal our physical bodies before we even know there's a problem. If we never seek to know what the dilemma was to begin with, we will never know the depth to which God can heal. The same goes for our emotional healing. If we never identify the full scope of our issues, we will never understand the level to which we were healed, and we won't have the resources God is longing to give us to encourage others to seek a similar healing.

We can experience freedom and wholeness after brokenness. God promises it and I can attest to it. I encourage you to take any broken part of your heart back to the Lord and allow Him, the Great Physician, to address the issue and administer healing.

11

Open Heart Surgery.

FORGIVENESS.

When most people hear this word, something inside them aches or twinges. It resonates with something deep that has most likely been suppressed or pushed down with neglect to process.

All of us at some point have been rejected, discarded, abused, hurt, abandoned, or denied. Because of this, every one of us is in a place where we must choose to forgive. Some wounds go so far back and are so deep we wonder if God can ever fully heal them. All I can say to this matter is that He will and can, but only if you let Him.

The pain of my broken family and marriage is no secret. My ex-husband made his sin a public display I was forced to walk through and navigate without warning. In my opinion, he became a different person in the process and didn't seem to care whose lives he was destroying or how his choices were affecting others. If there's anything I understand, it's rejection, abandonment, and hurt.

To this day, I look back to the whirlwind months after he left and remember the ache, turmoil, and agony I felt deep in my heart. Luckily, now it's only a distant memory.

The pain isn't as real and present as it once was. At the time, there was pain that was cultivating an energy charged by anger. This anger, quite honestly, is the fuel that helped me move out of my home in Ohio and into my parents' house in Pennsylvania, assist with running a conference for over 3000 women, and still manage the care of my daughter—all within a two week span of the man's departure.

In some ways, the energy from this anger was helping me to survive. I was able to be numb and plow through all that was necessary to transition out of my old life (all I knew) into an unknown 'normal.' I needed all the stamina I could get, but I found it was exhausting to maintain and I needed to let go.

I began to feel this nudging in my heart to allow God to take this pain and anger. It was too heavy and too much for my heart to hold onto.

I was walking around with my views tainted by my agony. I was hurting, and because of it I was constantly on guard to protect myself from any new trauma. I expected everyone I ever trusted and cared for to betray me in some way. My beliefs about people in general became jaded.

As a nurse, I tend to view things in medical analogies, and God has an odd way of relating to me in this way to speak truth and bring revelation and healing into my life. So bear with me as I walk you through my journey.

The way I began to see my situation was in terms of an initial trauma or injury to the skin. Brokenness, bleeding, and pain as a result of an incredible unforeseen blow. In an attempt to manage the immediate burden of bleeding and pain, the reality of the desperate need for medical attention went unrecognized. It's easy to get caught up in the how's and why's the trauma occurred and fail to realize the need for true healing and some assistance with the stitching (or closing) of the gaping wound.

I was trying to keep from bleeding all over my family and friends.

I tried covering my wound with smiles and productivity.

I thought if it was covered, cleaned up, and no one else was affected by it, then maybe it was healing and would be ok. Because time heals all wounds, right?

I didn't realize, even though my wound began to scab and heal over on the surface, the tissue underneath was still wide open and raw. Because I hadn't allowed God access to the wound, He wasn't able to do the necessary stitching to close it so it would heal properly. Now every time the wound was slightly touched, I felt the same excruciating pain. It was as though I was experiencing the initial blow all over again.

As time went on and new offenses occurred, the wound would easily reopen and the rawness underneath was revealed. There are only so many times that a wound can remain open or be reopened before infection sets in and wreaks havoc under the surface. This complicates the preexisting wound and adds a whole new layer to the problem and pain.

There's an adrenaline rush with any new injury that kicks in to assist with the survival of the immediate trauma. As that wears off, the reality of pain sinks in.

We are capable of surviving on this adrenaline for quite some time as we push through adversity. It's one thing to have the sting of the original wound, as well as the anger and frustration that goes with it. It's another to plow through it, not address what caused it, and just move forward while trying to prevent any damage that may occur in the future.

I became guarded and over-protective of my wound so I would never have to experience such angst ever again. What I didn't realize was my damage control didn't fix or heal my problem. By trying to manage on my own, I actually made matters worse. I didn't notice the underlying infection of bitterness and unforgiveness until I really allowed God access to all areas of my heart.

I'm grateful that this process came quick for me along my journey as I turned toward God in the moment my trauma occurred.

I listened to His voice for direction and guidance and was willing to obey His every word. I leaned on Him for strength and cried out to Him for peace.

The floods of grace in these moments were astounding. I was acutely aware of His constant presence. Because I stayed close to Him, He was steady to reveal all that needed to change. I also knew I could never feel this horrible ever again so I might as well surrender and allow Him to chisel away EVERYTHING in my heart that needed to go.

Years of painful experiences and layers of scar tissue needed to be cut away. If I was going to allow Him to address this most painful infection overwhelming my soul, then I figured it best to remain under the knife to do a complete work and healing in my heart. All offenses, all hurts, all brokenness were laid before Him to excise and—with a steady, gentle hand—remove for good.

I made a conscious decision to do all that was necessary to allow God to make me better because of my circumstances. I refused to become a victim of someone else's foolish choices and be defined by their mess.

Like any surgery, the pain of the immediate cutting to get below the surface to address the nagging problem is a new wave of pain unlike the one you have been experiencing prior. It's sharp, intense, and direct.

The difference is that it's intentional. You are surrendered to it, and you know it is coming. You also know your brokenness is in the hands of a trusted Surgeon, and you are confident the outcome and long term healing is going to be so much more beneficial to your daily living and health.

When I finally surrendered to this process and was willing to let God do this work in me, I had to set aside specific time for it to take place. I scheduled my surgery. I even picked the location and atmosphere that would be most conducive. I chose a quiet spot where I would have a significant amount of uninterrupted alone time.

I put on some worship music, most specifically a song titled, "You Know Me" that spoke the truth about God knowing the most intricate and ugly parts of our heart even if we choose not to acknowledge them before Him. In recognizing this, God also revealed to me that He saw the beauty under the surface, and by removing the yuck, He could allow the beauty to be seen.

When you are willing to allow God to perform this most intense heart surgery, be prepared to "ugly cry." I have never been one to cry a whole lot. I'm great at stuffing and stuffing until I explode. There were things I realized I never gave myself the permission or opportunity to properly grieve and process. I was long overdue for a good cry… about everything! This was my opportunity to let it all out while in the protective arms of God.

I cannot speak to anyone else's experience of forgiving. Initially, the experience of wading through layers of hurt and releasing every offense over to God was incredibly painful. I had to let go of any mental control I still wanted to maintain for hopes of future revenge, as if I could somehow mentally cause someone else to suffer remorse for their actions. It is laughable to think of it this way, but the truth is the enemy wants us to hold onto the bondage of unforgiveness. It's an unrealistic idea that the pain we feel daily will somehow be projected onto the person who caused it if we only hold on tight enough, and somehow, in releasing our pain we let the other person off the hook. This is a blatant lie!! At some point, we can all fall into this trap until we are shown that handing pain back over to God and choosing to forgive simply gives us the keys to let ourselves out of the prison our trauma forced us into. By letting go of our need to right our wrongs, we are unlocking the barred doors preventing us from a freed life.

I remember the heartrending emotional pain I endured. It felt physical as I released my desire to fight for justice. It was a deep and agonizing cutting away as I acknowledged every area of hurt and then allowed God to take it. Though I wasn't exempt from the pain of this experience, the Holy Spirit immediately met me with a comfort and a grace. Similar to an anesthesiologist, He was there to provide me with all the peace I needed to stay on the operating table.

When I came to a place where I was open and real enough before the Lord, knowing I had allowed Him all necessary access to my heart and there was nothing left to be removed, I expected to feel immediately free, whole, and full of joy. Instead, I felt raw and empty. I was disappointed. I had done exactly what I was supposed to, and I knew the weight I had been carrying was gone, so why didn't I feel better?

After removing all that was weighing me down, I was left with an open and gaping hole. Another process in my healing needed to take place in order for God to fully heal me. I had to let Him fill me with all HE wanted to be there. In my recovery, it was important for me to get proper nutrients and rest to provide what I needed to heal in a healthy way. I played worship music constantly, even as I slept, so my mind was constantly tuned in to an attitude of praise. I read my Bible as much as possible, feeding on all the truth and life I could.

After a few days of this, I didn't feel so empty, and I certainly wasn't in pain any more. I was able to hear God's voice more clearly and saw the world around me with His perspective. I was beginning to experience joy in the little things around me again.

My situation never changed, actually it got significantly worse for a season. But *I* had changed. I was better. I was whole. And with each new trauma, I was willing to bring it back to God for immediate repair of my heart. I can recall incredibly painful things that occurred during this time. But I can also remember just as clearly the steady hand of God's provision, and moments that were full of joy. Had I become stuck in my unforgiveness, my view would've been too jaded and clouded to see those moments and experience them fully.

Whether we feel like it or not, God's Word commands us to forgive others if we want our Heavenly Father to forgive us (Matthew 6:14,15). Forgiveness is an act of free will. It is also an act of obedience and will be greatly rewarded with peace, freedom, and true healing from past wounds. Giving the Lord access to all areas of your heart is an invaluable step in your walk with Him and reaps positive results in all avenues of your life.

12

Money DOES Grow on Trees.

"All I have needed thy hand hath provided…"[3]

A fter the visit to the doctor and before the scheduled surgery, I experienced days of intense pain and exhaustion. This made it difficult to complete regular daily tasks. It was especially taxing to carry the trash to the common receptacle and the laundry up and down the flight of stairs to our apartment, sitting in the small laundromat for several hours while it washed and dried.

I was able to get innovative with the trash, and I thank God for the wisdom He provides. I began setting aside all paper garbage to burn in our small fireplace we were blessed to have in the apartment. It helped keep utility costs down as the weather got cooler and also lessened the amount of trash we threw away. In another money-saving venture, I used plastic grocery bags to toss our trash in. This helped lighten the load of trash I took down the steps, and I would carry a bag or two out with me each time we left the apartment complex and toss it on our way. Sometimes our problems are overwhelming as a whole, but God is faithful to help us break it down into more manageable loads or provide resources to handle the task.

The laundry became a task too overwhelming to keep up with and was a growing frustration. A big factor adding to this was our two cats had also been traumatized by multiple moves. Their nervousness was displayed by peeing on our beds on a weekly basis. This resulted in me washing entire bedding sets—comforters, sheets and blankets—along with our normal loads of laundry. The bedding would take much longer to dry, and my body was so weak that sitting at the laundromat to wait for it was increasingly uncomfortable. Thus, I would end up hauling heavy, damp bedding up the flight of steps to the apartment and draping the bedding over doors and our balcony railing to dry it out.

I was processing heavy emotions, managing physical pain, and now carting all this heavy laundry. Facing an upcoming surgery, I knew I wasn't going to be able to keep up with doing the laundry this way. During my recovery, I was limited to lifting no more than five to ten pounds. And I certainly didn't want to have to ask my new friends for help in this department. I was fighting overwhelming emotions, and I finally reached a breaking point. Our apartment had washer and dryer hook ups, but without a job, I couldn't afford a set. With several baskets of dirty laundry piling up in front of me and too much physical pain to carry them to be washed, I threw my hands up in the air and told God I needed a washer and dryer. This was on a Wednesday morning. I knew that I had enough clean clothes to get me through the weekend, but then the cats decided to relieve themselves on the bedding again and I was done. I was feeling so sick I could barely get out of bed. All I could do with the bedding at the moment was soak it in the tub with detergent so it wouldn't get rancid. The conversation I had with God was out of exasperation and went something like this, "I need a washer and dryer, like, yesterday. I have no money to buy them and even if I did, I don't have the strength or energy to shop for them nor do I have a vehicle to pick them up even if I found a free set somewhere. I need you to fix this. I need a washer and dryer picked out and delivered to my apartment and set up. NOW!" Two days later, when I was so sick I was still in bed at eleven o'clock in the morning, I received a phone call from my mom. I struggled to compute what she was saying, but I managed to grasp she had shared my need with her Bible study group. One of the couples called her that morning to tell her God laid it on their hearts to provide me with the washer and dryer. They even found a local place minutes from my home and worked out a deal with the owner where I could pick out one of three possible sets within their price range. It would be delivered to my apartment and set up if I went that day to pick it out.

As grateful as I was for this miracle of provision, I was so sick and uncomfortable that rolling out of bed and getting dressed to go to the store was an overwhelming task. But sometimes we have to take some difficult steps to retrieve the miracle set before us. It was totally worth it.

By Monday afternoon I was washing all the bedding and clothes that had piled up. I had honestly never been so grateful to do laundry. I remember thanking God for this provision every time I put a new dirty load in. The beauty of it being in our apartment was I could lie down on the couch as the loads ran and my daughter could assist with changing the loads. Even though it's been several years since this miracle, there are still many times I will thank God for the ability to wash my laundry with my washer and dryer.

The surgery to remove the mass was finally scheduled for the week before Christmas. By the time I went through all the pre-op prep and had the surgery, the mass had grown from the size of an orange to the size of a grapefruit. My pain and exhaustion levels were increasing, and I was incredibly uncomfortable and ready to have this foreign thing removed.

As I went all this time without a job or source of steady

income, God continued to show me He was in control and was my Provider as random people and strangers from all over the country felt it on their heart to send us gift cards or checks. This steady provision sustained us, and we were not late on one payment all year!

My mom was able to fly down to be with me for my recovery, and new friends from church pitched in to help with Tali and bring us meals. We were overwhelmed with the love and support shown to us. God made sure we had all we needed.

For Christmas, I was able to get my daughter the exact gift she had asked for with a gift card to the exact store I could purchase it from. I was even able to get it online and have it delivered right to my doorstep so I didn't have to go out to shop while I recovered. I'm grateful she has not once had to feel the weight of not having enough. However, she was fully aware that I didn't have a job and I was intentional about sharing every blessing of provision that came our way. She could see how we steadily had what we needed and when it came. This included every single one of the Christmas gifts she got that year. She had told me prior to Christmas it was okay if she didn't get anything because she understood I didn't have a job. She was overwhelmed when she opened the items on her wish list and she asked how I could afford them. It was amazing to be able to share with her the ways God provided, not just for her needs, but for her desires.

Great is His FAITHFULNESS;
His mercies begin afresh every morning.
(Lamentations 3:23, emphasis added)

As December came to an end, I had just enough money to pay each bill and close out the month. However, the bills for January began piling up, and I wasn't sure how we were going to survive the month without the hopes of more 'blessed' Christmas cards.

Because I was still recovering from surgery and hadn't had the energy to un-decorate, we left the tree up until mid-January. This may be normal for some, but I tend to be a creature of habit and typically take it down the weekend right after New Years.

When we began taking our Christmas tree down, my daughter chose the task of removing the ornaments and placing them gently into a box one at a time. I was removing holiday wall hangings and garlands on the other side of the apartment when, suddenly, she started shouting across the room, "Mom! I found two dollars on the tree!"

Simultaneously, we were asking each other how it got there and if the other person stuck it in there as a joke. We both said "no" and as she began waving the two bills, I saw zeros and asked to see them. It appeared they were ten-dollar bills. As she brought them closer, I realized it was two ONE HUNDRED dollar bills!

We both started giggling and laughing as we continued to pack up the décor. She has often referenced that day stating, "If God can put money on our tree, He can do anything!"

And He did! He managed to get two one hundred-dollar bills onto our pre-lit blue spruce at the exact moment we were in need of another miracle! This was another one of those moments God strategically and deliberately blessed us in a way we couldn't deny His provision. He does that, ya know? He has ways of making it absolutely clear He is looking out for us and watching over us when we feel alone or insignificant.

You are NOT alone! You are NOT forgotten! He has you covered and cared for, even when you are feeling broken and lost. He will carry you when you're weak, comfort you when you're sad and abandoned, and provide for you when your bank account is empty. It may not come the way you expect. It will most likely come in a way you would LEAST expect. But it will be there, right when you need it.

You may be able to reflect, as I am, on Christmases past

with a grateful heart for a time when God carried and provided for you. You may also be in a similar desperate state of needing His steady hand of provision, wondering where He is right now. In either place, look up and begin to praise Him for what He has already done in your life and is about to do.

13

Stranger Blessings.

Is there an end to God's goodness or provision? Can we out-need God? Is there anything He can't do? Based on my experience, the answer to these three questions is "NO." Plain and simple, there is nothing too difficult for Him to handle.

On a Thursday afternoon, mid-January, I witnessed a tow company place an offensively large, neon yellow sticker on my car window stating if I didn't get my car registered in Georgia by the following Monday, which was a holiday, they would tow it. Basically, they were driving around looking for cars they could tow to make some money. It was irritating to me they found mine in the far lot of the apartment complex.

In all the craziness of moving, getting settled, and having surgery, I had overlooked the expired registration. The next day, I rushed to get it all taken care of to avoid having my car towed. Come to find out, the process of registering your vehicle in Georgia is like a cruel fraternity initiation, and I had one day to complete everything before the holiday weekend.

Thirty-five dollars was dropped on a new driver's license, twenty dollars for a required emission test, and sixty for Georgia plates and registration. The final bomb was the taxes they charged on the value of your vehicle, even if it was purchased in another state and taxes were previously paid. Because my car, at the time, was newer and hadn't depreciated much, the total due was over fifteen hundred dollars!!

I started crying right there at the tag office. The woman said I could pay half then, and they would hold onto my title until I paid the other half within the year. But even half the amount due was what I needed to pay my rent that month!

Back in August, before the second debacle, I felt God impress upon my heart to use half of whatever anyone gave me for my monthly expenses and put the other half in my savings. I didn't have any idea what it was supposed to be for. Even as other needs arose, I considered it to be untouchable. It was easy to agree to such a deal since I figured half of nothing was nothing.

Little by little, money kept being sent to us. With each need that arose, God provided twice the amount. Half went to pay the bills and the other half went into savings, as God instructed. People I hadn't heard from in years felt it on their heart to send us money. Checks from complete strangers, friends of friends who had heard my story, kept rolling in.

We were able to live modestly on half of what was coming in. I was frugal and extremely careful with my spending. All the while, I was trusting God with this steady provision because I still had no consistent salary.

That month, I also had to get four new tires for my car due to severe lack of tread on the front two and I ended up getting a flat tire as well. Six hundred and something dollars later, plus close to nine hundred for the registration process, I had burned through what was set aside in my savings account. God knew the needs that would arise, and He instructed me to prepare for them without me understanding why. I'm so grateful He had taught me to trust Him and hear His voice so I was prepared for this. My obedience was paying off.

With the seven hundred fifty dollars I still owed before me, I began praying God would provide a two-thousand-dollar-miracle to replenish what had been used for the initial tax payments and give provision to pay off the rest of the owed amount so I could get my title back. I had only three other people praying specifically for this, one being my mother. One month later, I got a phone call from my mom, who spoke at a women's event in another state that weekend.

She briefly shared how, through my experience, she felt compelled to launch a single moms ministry in Pennsylvania. Before she left the event, a woman from the audience approached her. This woman said she felt it on her heart to give me money and handed my mom an envelope. She told my mom she made the check out to her because she didn't even know my name. She just felt it on her heart to give.

She asked my mom to cash it and give it to me, hoping it would be a blessing. She also mentioned God had told her an exact amount to give me. Because of the large amount, she had to run the idea by her husband. His response was, "If God is telling you to do this, I'm not standing in your or His way."

When my mom called me to share the news of this and the amount of the check, I literally started laughing out of shock, joy, and gratitude. It was written for exactly two thousand dollars. I laughed for several hours after. The provision of God was so blatant!

I don't underestimate God anymore. He has proven He is my steady Provider, my faithful Father and my deliverer of grace. The blessings we received from strangers that kept us alive are unbelievable. He truly managed to amaze us on a regular basis. I learned no need was too great for Him. All I had to do was ask. As I face new or different challenges, I approach Him with confidence that He will surely provide. He certainly hasn't failed me yet.

Times of doubt or uncertainty have definitely had their day. But constant waves of provision, as I needed them, gave me the opportunity for my trust in Him to be rebuilt. Even though God wasn't the one to walk out on me, I felt betrayed and abandoned by Him for allowing me to get into an unfaithful relationship in the first place. I questioned why He allowed me to ever meet that man, let alone marry him, love him, and trust him. Where was God to protect me from pledging my life to him? I wrestled with this for only a short while because God was faithful to answer me right away. I needed to resolve this line of questioning before my daughter began asking the same questions.

He was there. He was there when I felt the Holy Spirit confirm this was the person I was supposed to marry. He was there on my wedding day. He was there all the times He had given that man the opportunity to change his course and turn his heart back to the Lord. He was there when I gave birth to my daughter and He imparted a plan and purpose to her life. He was there when life was good and when it was not. He was always there.

And He still is. No matter what comes my way, He is there. He will comfort me and guide me, provide for me and protect me. He will prove Himself faithful when the rest of the world is not.

I'll never forget the moment my sweet girl questioned the sovereignty of God. So innocent and honest, she verbalized what we were all trying desperately to understand. I was grateful I had wrestled my own thoughts out with the Lord. I was also grateful the wisdom of the Holy Spirit broke into my mind and I allowed myself to speak His truths in spite of the brokenness in my heart. We had only moved into my parents' home a matter of weeks prior to her approaching me at the kitchen table. I picked her up and set her on my lap. She looked at me with those deep brown eyes and asked, "Why did God allow you to marry daddy, if He knew he was going to leave?"

If it wasn't for the grace of God and the leading of the Holy

Spirit, I would not have answered this question well. Using my own human strength, I would've probably done more damage to this little heart or not have an answer that could satisfy such a need for understanding.

She was hurting, too. She needed answers, too. At seven years of age, she was only beginning to learn how to hear from God on her own. Then her whole world was turned upside down and everything she thought she knew was disrupted. She struggled to grasp what was true in the midst of chaos and brokenness. So did I. I knew if I wasn't hearing from God and getting answers from Him, I would never be able to provide answers for her.

Without a thought in my mind, the words flew out of my mouth. "If I never married your dad, you wouldn't be here. God obviously wanted to make sure that you were born because He has a very important plan for your life. You were the best gift I could've ever received and the best thing to come from marrying your dad. You were worth it."

Though I was shocked by my ability to answer her in such certainty, I also realized I truly believed the words that I was speaking. This was something God had written on my heart for me to carry through the turmoil. Just as much as she needed to see purpose through the pain, so did I.

Whether it was physical, mental, or emotional needs that surfaced, God was consistent and intentional with His provision. He proves He is truly good and I trust Him. By continuing to keep our hearts and minds focused on Him during all seasons of life, we are able to see the truth He wants to reveal to us along the way. We don't always get the answer to the question "Why?", but we will receive His perspective. This is a priceless gift when we are wading through chaos. Don't try to find answers in the rubble and dust swirling about you. Look up, above it all. Seek Him first.

14

Am I Enough?

LOVE.

As a single woman, or someone who has had their heart broken, sometimes hearing or seeing that word stings. We all desire to be loved, cherished, and adored. We long for someone to see beauty and value in us. We want to be validated, encouraged, and cared for. For some wackadoo reason, we think a MAN is the only way this can happen. I'm not sure whether we can blame society or Hallmark, but somewhere along our journey we've adopted this belief as truth.

We tend to live in constant disappointment when our reality doesn't line up with our expectations. Our purpose in life is encouraged to be driven by a whimsical, magical, romantic adventure. Without it, our lives are considered meaningless and flat. This false belief must be addressed and combated with TRUTH.

Often the sense something is missing is a reflection of the failure to realize what we have or what IS.

We feel as though WE are not enough. That we don't have what it takes to be completely wonderful and whole all on our own.

That our lives are not significant and valuable without a significant other who values us.

That we are unable to bless those around us with the little we have to offer.

I'd like to remind you that God does His best work with situations that appear to not be "enough." Too few loaves and fish, empty oil jars, shortage of wine, illness, death—these are what He tends to use to reveal the depths of His love and genuine care for our individual needs. He can use whatever we have to offer Him and do more with us than we could ever imagine.

Allow God to bring you to a place of wholeness in Him. If you are able to live a whole and fulfilled life alone, the joy of having someone to share it with is more like an added blessing. You relieve that person from the responsibility of meeting your needs, and you are less likely to be disappointed in your marriage and other relationships as well.

Seek out truth for your value and identity in Christ. Choose to hear God's heart and perspective of you. Meditate on it daily until you've replaced every false belief of yourself and you are living your life with the freedom of knowing your worth.

We are loved by our Heavenly Father.
"See what great love the Father has lavished on us, that we should be called children of God! And that is what we are!" (1 John 3:1, NIV)

We are forgiven.
"You, Lord, are forgiving and good, abounding in love to all who call to you." (Psalm 86:5, NIV)

We have hope.
"Let us hold unswervingly to the hope we profess, for he who promised is faithful." (Hebrews 10:23, NIV)

We are beautiful.
"I praise you because I am fearfully and wonderfully made; your works are wonderful, I know that full well." (Psalm 139:14, NIV)

We were created on purpose.
"For we are God's handiwork, created in Christ Jesus to do good works, which God prepared in advance for us to do." (Ephesians 2:10, NIV)

By believing God's truth about ourselves, we are able to see what doesn't line up in the world around us. Our perspective shifts and we recognize where our beliefs were skewed in the past.

When we find ourselves laden with disappointment, fear, and anxiety about what we see in our lives, go back to the Word of God and meditate on what is true. It takes habitual training to take a step back from certain situations and glean from the Lord before reacting or responding. Keep practicing. You won't get it right every time. We are certainly not perfect, but we can take daily steps in the right direction.

Over time, you will develop a clear understanding of God's love for you, His purpose for you, and how He sees you as His cherished son or daughter. You will begin to walk in the confidence of this truth and realize that all the validation, affirmation, acceptance, and love you ever needed comes from God. You will realize your value through His eyes and understand His purpose for your life without requiring the influence or opinion of another person.

15

A Little Perspective.

The Valentine's Day (otherwise known as Single's Awareness Day) immediately following my ex-husband's departure was by far one of the worst I've ever experienced. The holiday seemed to amplify my feelings of rejection, pain, and loss with all the commercialism of romance and emphasis on relationships.

I was faced with some important decisions during this season that determined how I walked out my journey. To be quite honest, hiding in my bedroom at my parents', remaining in my PJs for days on end, eating ice cream, and sulking was definitely my most natural choice of response. However, I was able to think forward a bit to realize the waste of time and lack of effectiveness this would have on my life. I was determined to rise above the mess and not let it turn me into someone I never desired to be.

I was also acutely aware my daughter was watching my every move. She was going to learn how to walk through adversity with grace and peace, but only if I showed her. With each day I chose to get out of bed, every moment I pressed in to build relationships and interact with others, I was being watched. I came to realize it wasn't just my daughter observing my choice to consistently cling to God, but family and friends were also paying close attention.

I suppose enough people have seen a marriage crumble before their eyes to have certain assumptions as to how most usually handle the collapse. They also know how they would probably handle the same betrayal and rejection I had been subject to, typically including the "Recluse Response" of jammies and ice cream. So, when they would see me out and about with my makeup on and my hair brushed, I received many shocked responses. Some were actually quite comical.

I knew as Valentine's Day was approaching I needed to be proactive in how I addressed the potential wave of heartache on this day. I decided immediately I wasn't going to tackle it alone! I had connected with two single women at my parents' church since I moved back home and was pretty sure they had no desire to be alone that evening either.

I invited them over for an "All Things Red" dinner. The three of us collaborated on the meal and each made special red treats to munch on throughout the evening. One of the girls even picked up a video for us to watch. My daughter especially loved decorating for the evening and setting the table with the "fancy stuff Nana keeps in the glass cabinet." We made it our own special celebration. We talked and laughed. For a while I was able to forget why I was celebrating that evening without my husband.

What I want to encourage, for Valentine's Day and every holiday, is to embrace the moments that could potentially cause added pain or feelings of loss and find ways to celebrate the people in your life God has placed there for you to love. You may have siblings or parents, aunts, uncles, nieces, nephews, or friends in your life who you can choose to pour your love into. Some of them may be a little more difficult to love than others or be super quirky and difficult to connect with, but seek God for special ways you can show them love. It doesn't have to be some grand gesture or cause financial strain to make a point. It may be a sacrifice of time or energy to be present in their lives and embrace times together as family.

If you don't live in close proximity to your immediate family, or it is necessary for you to limit time with them due to dysfunction, choose to get involved in your local church and create a family there. You have to be a friend to make a friend! Just because you are the new girl or guy doesn't mean you can't be the one inviting people over or initiating a get-together. Get involved in a group or area to serve in order to connect with others right away. Start to open your eyes to see the world and people around you.

Stop and think about it, maybe even make a list. There are probably numerous people you can truly share God's love with at this time in your life. Without thinking of what or who you are lacking, embrace the people right in front of you.

Choose to enjoy life and the lives of those around you. Choose to see your blessings and not what you lack. Choose to bless others in spite of your own feelings. Choose to celebrate love.

And choose to only eat ice cream in your jammies if you are hosting a slumber party and you have plenty of friends or nieces and nephews to join you!

For those of you still struggling to embrace this season of life in a positive way, chin up! There is no need to beat yourself up for feeling way too sorry for yourself…this is counterproductive. There is also no need to stay in this sulky, feel-sorry-for-yourself state. Today, let's make a choice to not dwell on the shoulda, coulda, woulda and let's embrace every positive element present in our daily lives.

Fix your thoughts on what is TRUE, and HONORABLE,
and RIGHT, and PURE, and LOVELY, and ADMIRABLE.
Think about things that are excellent and worthy of praise.
(Philippians 4:8b, emphasis added)

We need to be intentional to think of such things. Our minds quickly get clouded by all the negativity that comes our way, and we lose sight of what is good. If you haven't done so already, take a moment today to make a list of all the blessings right in front of you. Then, list all of the ways you can bless others and who could be the recipient. I encourage you to do this often, especially if you struggle as I do to keep a positive perspective on what you have. Taking the step beyond gratitude and being aware of areas we have MORE than enough will deepen our level of trust in our Provider and shift our focus to the needs of others.

It takes time and a bit of mental work to retrain your brain to see things in this light. When we dwell on all that's gone wrong or is going wrong, we can easily get our minds stuck there. In turn, we may fail to venture into a new opportunity out of fear.

We may find ourselves anxious about our future because we are still staring at our past.

We will stop encouraging those around us to be courageous because we've given up in our own fight.

What we choose to dwell on will directly affect our choices and actions.

If you are unable to see what is true, honorable, right, pure, lovely, and admirable, spend time in God's Word and let it be a daily reminder. Ask Him for His perspective of people and situations.

16

Letting Go.

I grew up singing the beautiful song, "I Surrender All." You know, the one that goes *"All to Jesus, I surrender, all to Him I freely give."*[4]

I never really took into account what that meant. Surrendering all seems so nice. The idealistic approach to Christianity of "Letting Go and Letting God."

No more worries. No more stress. Be Blessed and Nothing Less. Right?

That's a lovely idea. And there is an element of truth when you finally arrive at the place of peace and rest in Christ, but getting there is often PAINFUL!

Every New Year I think about how so many are trying to establish new and better ways of doing things: get organized, eat better foods, exercise, stick to a budget. These are all great things to add to our lives and are certainly important for living well-balanced. But in order for anything new to have a place to stay, we must remove what was there previously that was tripping us up.

Out with the OLD, in with the NEW!

I learned this especially as I was trying to find space in my daughter's bedroom for all the new toys and gifts she received for Christmas. We were forced to go through her old toys, sort through what she still played with, and get rid of anything broken or unwanted, or missing parts.

For my daughter, this was an extremely difficult process. She is sentimental and had recently experienced tremendous amounts of loss. This made it difficult to let go of anything with a memory or might have a potential use in the future. We had to take our time with each item and weigh out its value for life at that moment.

Was it something she would still play with when the new stuff came in?

As we went further into the process, it became easier and easier for her to give away or toss anything she no longer wanted or had simply turned into junk over the years. Her focus shifted from trying to hold onto what was, to making room for NEW.

We may want an abundance of peace, joy, prosperity, and love, but we have to make room for it. These things can't take their place if worry, fear, anger, and unforgiveness have settled in. This surrender of all the unnecessary can be difficult and painful. Sometimes it requires us to be willing to go back to that hurt, the initial cause of the pain, look at it, process it, and lay it before the Lord. Hand it over to Him. Our little hearts were not meant to carry the weight of such grief and pain. He is ready and willing to take it from us if we are willing to let go.

Whether you are trading bad habits for healthy ones, or exchanging sorrow for joy, surrender it all to God and allow Him to help you with the clean up.

In order to receive all the NEW that God has for us, we need to be willing to lay down and clean out anything that is just taking up space in our lives and in our hearts. It takes an act of surrender before the Lord to allow Him to chisel away all the things that we may feel are necessary to be there. He may be the only one who can see the NEW that's coming and He knows where you'll need 'room' for it.

For I am about to do something new.
See, I have already begun! Do you not see it?
I will make a pathway through the wilderness.
I will create rivers in the dry wasteland.
(Isaiah 43:19)

17

Mama Said:
There'll Be Days Like This.

I finally reached a point in the journey of my new single life and single motherhood where I wasn't working hard to simply survive. After two years of feeling as though I was treading water just to stay above the waves and catch occasional breaths, I was starting to feel like I could rest a bit and breathe again with less difficulty and struggle. The stormy sky began to part and reveal brighter days, and the steady waves of challenges had calmed.

PEACE.

I was looking forward to establishing some new traditions that Christmas with my daughter: baking cookies and decorating together, shopping, and attending holiday parties. I was embracing our new family unit of two and settling in to finding joy in our every day. There were also some potential blessings hanging in the balance and I found myself looking forward.

HOPE.

And then WHAM! In a week's time all I was looking forward to, hoping for, praying for, and planning for fell apart and I came UNDONE!

I had barely returned home and unpacked from a Thanksgiving trip with my family and I landed myself in the ER again! Severe pain onset quickly and had me driving myself (like a mad woman) to the hospital. Imagine Madea meets Mario Andretti. Curbs were jumped; stop signs and red lights were suddenly merely suggestions, as I was doubling over.

After many hours and multiple tests at the hospital, I was told I needed to go home, rest, take my meds to render myself unconscious and keep the pain at bay until I could be scheduled for surgery sometime in the New Year.

I sarcastically thought to myself, *"That's EXACTLY what I had on my wish list this year! Another surgery!"*

After having surgery the year before, right before Christmas, spending the time sore and medicated, I was hoping this year would be different. Better.

Unfortunately, this wasn't the only thing derailing my week and subsequently my thought process and emotions. On top of this abrasive new reality landed a disappointment that even now, years later, I am trying to figure out and understand the 'hows' and 'whys' of. I've resolved I may never have the answer.

Sometimes we are handed things we aren't meant to handle and figure out on our own. This is where the Enemy likes to step in and cause you to question your hope, rob your peace, and demolish any joy you thought you had or ever would have.

Once your mind starts taking a trip to Doomsville, every little thing that creeps up becomes overwhelming and can turn on the waterworks, or stir up frustration and anger in seconds. The rest of my week became a "Series of Unfortunate Events" which, by the grace of God, I can now look back on with a little humor. However, in the moment, not so much!

Throughout that week, I was trying to manage pain, extreme nausea, doctor visits and scheduling, sporadic fevers, and still care for my daughter. I was exhausted, miserable, disappointed, and feeling sorry for myself. Two days after my eventful trip to the ER, I woke up in the morning knowing that was the day the pity party was happening. I was sad, and in my sadness, ridiculousness ensued.

I made the effort that morning to make some coffee and get something to eat (which took a lot out of me). I managed to drop my plate of food and half of my eggs, which became a scavenger hunt for my two cats. I cut my losses, headed to the couch with now one severely scrambled egg and cup of coffee and prepared to get situated comfortably (this also felt like work).

Just as I found the optimum position to sit and eat in minimal pain, I picked up my coffee. As I went to sip, realized the cup was nowhere near my mouth as the hot liquid poured all down the front of me!

Later that day, a friend brought groceries and came to help with some things around the house. While she was here, I managed to cut my finger on the kitchen counter top. Don't ask! These things happen, and it's always nonsensical. It was a deep cut that took a long time to stop bleeding, layering more pain on top of existing pain. One more reason to pout.

That evening, my stomach took a sudden turn for the worse as a result of taking pain meds. I cannot adequately describe the thoughts and feelings one experiences when the toilet one is desperate for is found clogged with an excessive amount of toilet paper and water is filled to the brim and not draining. Panic is a word that comes to mind. I love my little girl, but oh my! I did not have the physical ability to be patient in that moment. I also faced the daunting reality that we did not own a plunger! **Desperate times call for desperate measures!**

I quickly grabbed whatever random household products I could find to help break up the wads of paper. Draino, baking soda and vinegar were all dumped in. Result: lots of bubbles but no breakthrough! My daughter and I went on a rapid hunt through the house for random long stemmed items that could help us on our quest. In case you find yourself in a similar predicament, crowbars and mini blind open-closer wands do NOT work to unclog a toilet. The classic and unfailing toilet brush came through for me that evening and are, thankfully, cheap enough to replace.

Needless to say, after the final ordeal of the day, I was EXHAUSTED and feeling quite sore. The last thing I attempted to do was take a near-empty plastic lemonade container out of the fridge to be washed. As soon as I picked it up, I dropped it on the hard tile floor, and a huge chunk cracked like glass and the remaining contents spilled and splashed everywhere. I was SO DONE!!

I could barely bend down to clean the mess up and throw my container away. I knew I needed to sit, rest and not touch another thing in the house. Unlike King Midas, nothing I was touching was turning to gold. I was dangerously destructive.

I fixed myself a cup of tea (which I spilled a good portion of on the kitchen floor I just cleaned) and went directly toward my favorite spot on the couch. Just as I removed my slippers, sat down, and propped my feet up, my cat came over and vomited inside my slipper!

So we're not giving up. How could we! Even though
on the outside it often looks like things are falling apart on
us, on the inside, where God is making new life, not a day
goes by without his unfolding grace.
(2 Corinthians 4:16, MSG)

The following week, I had friends come to help my daughter and I decorate for Christmas. They made our home feel warm and cozy and our hearts full. I had been disappointed I wasn't going to be able to physically do this, and it turned out that receiving their help made me realize how blessed I was to have them in my life.

The night before they arrived, another friend brought dinner and came to clean and prep my house for Decorating Day. This friend also helped us to do our usual Christmas cookie baking that I was afraid my daughter and I would miss out on.

There were several others who made us meals or came to help, making me realize how genuinely loved we truly are. Sometimes, friends, you don't realize who and what there is around you until you find yourself in a pit!

LOVE.

Navigating through those dark, lonely places is where we find God's grace, provision, and rest. Without them, we would never have a need for it and never learn how to tap into it. In our desperation, if we are looking in the right place and surrender ourselves before the Lord, we can actually see and experience His blessings.

Between Thanksgiving and New Years, most people are busy planning the perfect holiday party. I am personally aware that many are struggling to connect with the world around them because they're weighed down and buried under the disappointments and pressures of life. For others, this time of year may stir up painful memories from childhood or Christmases past. Instead of Decking the Halls and making things merry and bright, there are thoughts of throwing those Silver Bells across the room and ordering shipments of coal to be delivered to the doorstep of those who've pained you (true story!). We can't forget to mention the turmoil that rages within when the song, "It's the Most Wonderful Time of the Year!" starts playing.

As I mentioned earlier, I faced a series of difficult experiences in a short period of time that started to lead me down a dangerous emotional path. Too many disappointing and stressful things to process at once can often lead to an overload of thoughts and feelings that bog us down. I got caught up into the downward spiral of negative thinking and sadness. What I learned this time, as I was sinking into the pit of despair, was how to recognize when you're on your way down and what to do to climb back out.

I knew the moment I woke up one morning I was going to have an unscheduled Pity Party. I was able to tell from the tone of my thoughts.

Immediately I knew that, like any good party, it's best if you invite friends!

Not to join me in my misery, but to pray for me as I began my pouting session. I have an arsenal of prayer warriors who, at the words "please pray," are on it! No questions asked. Align yourself with such people, and learn to immediately utilize them in moments such as these.

Be such a person. Recognize when life begins to happen to us, we often can't handle it on our own, and we need to call in for reinforcements.

A good Pity Party also requires a quality venting session.

You need to process those emotions and Let. Them. Out!! What you are feeling is typically valid and justifiable. But I've learned the hard way that not everyone can handle the heavy emotions of others. The key is finding a safe place to vent. For some, the safest place may be a journal.

I am blessed to have a friend who lets me text crazy rants throughout the day. She checks in with me later to see how I'm processing it all and provides perspective when needed. Most of the time, she knows I just need to get it out and doesn't feel the need to adjust my emotions. Such a friend is a rare and true gift. Reading back through the string of texts I sent during my pity party was almost entertaining, and I'm sure she laughed at me half of the time. Until you find one of these friends, learn to be one of these friends.

Every party needs good music!

Music has the ability to set a mood for those listening, so choose wisely. If you can sense the emotional downward spiral beginning, make the difficult choice to fill your home and your heart with praise to God. You may not feel like it, but we can't operate through life governed by our feelings. Sometimes we need to take those steps in the right direction and make conscious decisions to adjust our thought process and emotions. Be intentional to list all of the things that are right or okay in your life, things you can be grateful for. There has to be something! If you have a radio or CD player to listen to or a device to read this book on, you have something tangible to be thankful for.

With perspective and a WHOLE lot of prayer, I was pulled out of that yucky pit and stopped seeing all I was losing and lacking. I started to readjust my sights on what I STILL had right in front of me and was able to find strength to praise God for it.

It's hard to praise at a pity party. The mindset has to change and what you're uttering out of your mouth must shift from complaints to gratitude. But I can tell you from personal experience that it can be done.

When you go through deep waters, I will be with you.
When you go through rivers of difficulty, you will not drown.
When you walk through the fire of oppression, you will not
be burned up; the flames will not consume you.
For I am the Lord, your God, the Holy One of Israel, your Savior.
(Isaiah 43:2-3a)

18

The Present.

The first year I moved to Georgia, after the first surgery, I began attending a weekly group designed to walk women through healing from the effects of infidelity in marriage. This group became one of my lifelines, and I met amazing women who are still an integral part of my life today. Every week, we worked through another layer of pain that needed to be addressed and healed. This was neither easy nor fun. It hurt most of the time, but it was so worth it to take this path toward freedom. I'm grateful for the girls who stuck with me on my ugly days and embraced me when I was falling apart. These women are some of the strongest, bravest, and most genuine people I will ever know.

Toward the end of the second year, I was asked to write out a vision statement for my life. We were encouraged to spend the necessary time with the Lord to hear His heart for the direction He was taking our lives, then write it out in one or two sentences and draw a picture to go along with it. I was confident with the writing part of it, but knew that my picture would look as though I didn't pass

Kindergarten.

All throughout that week, I was intentionally seeking God for some form of communication or direction on how I could articulate His vision for my life. I was looking for a revelation, mission, or mantra to carry me or propel me forward. A couple of years ago it would've consisted of something like, *"By the time I'm 30, I will…"* or *"In the next 5 years…"* or even, *"Some day…"* Afterwards I would feel as though God had dropped those dreams in my heart and placed that call on my life, so I would then begin doing everything in my power to cause these goals to come about. I'd begin orchestrating things and making decisions at present in preparation for a future that wasn't even on the radar. I'd work tirelessly toward a goal that would constantly end in disappointment as it didn't come about in my timing.

I wanted it to be different this time.

I longed for a specific dream or vision I was certain was only coming from God, and I knew for sure He was promising to fulfill.

Every time I sat down with that blank sheet of paper waiting to be filled with this amazing new revelation God was about to bring me to…I had nothing. Me, a writer, had no words to put on a blank white page of possibility.

The truth was I hadn't allowed myself to dream in a long time. All the dreams I had, that had been fulfilled, had also been taken away. Dreaming, for me, has only led to painful disappointment. I realized grief and fear began to rise as I was seeking God for direction on this assignment. I was forced to deal with some unresolved anger I had toward Him. There was certainly some lack of trust, as well, in believing He would fulfill my dreams for the future, and I realized I had stopped praying for desires I had on my heart out of fear of being disappointed when they never came to be.

I also know dreams and plans, in the past, kept me looking

ahead but failing to see or fully enjoy what was right in front of me. I was always looking to the next great thing God would bring along or amazing ministry I would someday be a part of or lead. I was in a constant battle between contentment with what I had and making plans for my future.

All that has changed now. I never dreamed or imagined I'd be where I am today—a divorced, single mom living on a wing and a prayer. I also never imagined I would ever see the miracles God has performed for us over the past five years. Nor did I EVER, in a million years, picture myself writing, speaking, and traveling on a regular basis! All that is happening for me now is a result of me blindly stepping forward in obedience to how God is directing me, and the doors that continue to keep opening have me constantly shaking my head in amazement.

The morning the assignment was due, I stared down at that blank white page again and realized I had no vision or goal for my future. I'm better off sticking to the plan of following in blind obedience and watching the amazing things God does. I sat before Him with my hands open and said, *"I surrender my plans and my dreams and my desires and lay them at your feet."* I don't know what lies ahead for me, but I know if I let Him lead, I will continue to be pleasantly surprised.

Unfortunately, this open-handed, laying down of dreams still had me staring at a blank page. All I could hear God whispering to me was, *"Be present."*

So what did this kindergarten-level artist draw?

A present!! That's right, a simple box with a bow on it.

I was finally able to articulate the vision I feel God has for my life right now and I truly believe it is one He has for all of us. "To stay present. To focus on what is right in front of us. To not worry about what could be, what was, or what will be, but to enjoy what is."

When I sat in my group that week and saw everyone's beautiful pictures (some members are clearly artists) and heard the amazing visions God impressed on their hearts for their lives, I started to feel a bit insecure about my little gift box and simple statement. Yet, as I shared, I realized how profound it was for me, the type-A, plan-ahead-guru, to be uttering such words for my life. For once, even with all the broken and messy pieces from shattered dreams, I am okay to be right where God has me. I am at peace to go in whatever direction He leads. And I can trust it will be much better than anything I try to muster up on my own.

As I have reflected back on my sad drawing of the little gift box, I realize, it is a true representation of a present He is giving me for right now. It is an absolute blessing to be able to enjoy all God has placed in my life at the moment. There is peace in not feeling like I need to have it all figured out or be planning for when something new may come along. I can just enjoy today for what it is, and I am much more aware of little blessings that come my way because I'm paying attention to what is in front of me.

It is very difficult to receive gifts when your hands are closed into tight fists. Unwrapping them is exceptionally challenging. So many of life's experiences can leave us clinging tightly to what is left: the remnants of the past. We may fear letting go because we don't want to be left with nothing. I was there. I held tightly to my broken pieces, at times, because I didn't trust there could be anything better than what I was clinging to.

It is a struggle to take hold of anything new with our hands clasped around something else. It's difficult to believe we could ever have better than what we find for ourselves. Some of us are survivors; we've had to make a way for ourselves and care for ourselves because no one else did. Some of us can't imagine what it would feel like to not have to be so self-reliant. I couldn't.

But the gifts God wants to give us can't be received unless

we open our hands. We will never know how secure and at peace we can feel until we let go. There are so many amazing adventures, plans, and blessings ready for us to take hold of, but we need to lay aside our expectations and how we plan to bring them about. We don't need to have it all figured out. We don't need to know how it's going to work or what the end result will be. We don't need to fear or be anxious about our future.

Just like the box of faith—filled with provision—that I was handed in the midst of my mess, choose to open your hands and your heart to the gift of faith that God wants to hand you today. Faith to believe that your story isn't over. Faith to believe that He is your Redeemer, your Provider, your Restorer, your Defender, and your Healer.

Take hold of the gift of faith and
believe with God you will always have
Just Enough.

Notes.

1   Merriam-Webster Dictionary. "Definition of debacle." Merriam-Webster.com. Last updated July 24, 2018. https://www.merriam-webster.com/dictionary/debacle.

2   Spafford, Horatio. "When Peace, Like a River." Hymnary. org, accessed July 20th, 2018. https://hymnary.org/text/when_peace_like_a_river_attendeth_my_way.

3   Chisolm, Thomas. "Great is Thy Faithfulness." Hope Publishing Co., Carol Stream, IL, 1921.

4   Van De Venter, Judson. "I Surrender All." Hymnary.org, accessed August 1, 2018. https://hymnary.org/text/all_to_jesus_i_surrender.

Acknowledgements.

For my mom – My pillar of prayer. Continuously petitioning our Heavenly Father on my behalf and watching Him move mountain after mountain.

For my dad – My steady supporter and a true example of a father and papa. His love for us is tangible.

For Natalia – She's taken this journey with me, has seen God's miraculous provision and has walked with grace and peace through every valley. She is a joy to my heart.

For Pastor and his wife, Terry – Encouragement in the deep end of the pit. They not only helped me practically, but they embraced my weary soul. They saw me beyond the broken mess of the moment and invested in my life.

For Jessica – There are not enough quality words to adequately express my deep level of love and appreciation for this friendship and sisterhood. Her faithfulness has been an anchor and a source of strength. She is irreplaceable!

For Tiffany – For the love of coffee and all that is sweet in this world, she is so dear to my heart. She caffeinates my life! God knew I needed someone who I could communicate strictly in Gifs to.

For Crystal – For providing a haven for my grieving heart. Her friendship welcomed me like a warm blanket over shivering shoulders. She surrounded me with love. I will cherish her always.

For the Giver (anonymous or known) – Everyone who mailed a check, gave me a gift card (or two), bought us a meal, sent us a gift... their obedience was my answer to prayer. Not a day goes by when I don't think of you with gratitude. You helped us survive and were used by God to bring hope and provision when we needed it most.

For the Broken, Messy Hearts that desperately long for healing and acceptance – You are loved, cherished and adored by your Heavenly Father.

About the Author.

Jennie Puleo considers her most important title to be 'mother.' It's always been her dream job. She considers it an honor to be called "Natalia's mom." Fostering and adoption has been on her heart for years and recently more children have been filling her home again.

Other titles Jennie currently holds are registered nurse, executive assistant, international speaker, and President of Live Restored, Inc.

Jen has always had a deep love for the Lord and her desire to serve and obey Him has carried her through so many of life's chaotic circumstances. The loss of children, abandonment of spouse, chronic illness, multiple surgeries; there are so many times and places where God has met her in the middle of a storm! It is now her passion and purpose to share all God has done in and through her by speaking and writing...and on occasion sharing God's love with a random stranger at a grocery store or in a doctor's office.

She currently lives with her daughter, Natalia, and two sweet kitties, Ebony and Padme', just outside Charlotte, North

Carolina. Jennie and Talia are often seen exploring historical sites or museums and making their own adventures in the world around them. They both love to travel and, as Jennie's self-proclaimed personal assistant, Talia enjoys traveling with Jennie as she speaks throughout the country and abroad. They have seen God provide for them in miraculous ways over the past six years and are eager to tell someone about the goodness of God.

You can learn more about Jennie at LiveRestored.net, on Facebook through her "Jennie Puleo Page," or contact her at liverestoredinc@gmail.com where she welcomes any questions, comments, or requests for speaking engagements.

31847197R00076

Made in the USA
Columbia, SC
10 November 2018